PROMPT
ENGINEERING
BIBLE

3 IN 1

Join and Master the AI Revolution | Profit Online with
GPT-4 & Plugins for Effortless Money Making!

ROBERT E. MILLER

TABLE OF CONTENTS

INTRODUCTION

I find it both fascinating and thrilling that we are at the precipice of an era where Artificial Intelligence (AI) is no longer a distant concept from science fiction but a vivid reality of our everyday lives. Similar to how nutrition science brought us closer to understanding the intricate connection between food and health, AI is leading us to an understanding of how intertwined humans and technology have become. The age of the Fourth Industrial Revolution, as it's often referred to, heralds a time when digital, physical, and biological worlds have begun to converge, changing our lives and businesses in ways we could only dream of a few decades ago.

The quintessence of this revolution, as you've probably guessed, is AI and, more specifically, the powerful machine learning models, such as GPT-4, that have opened up a cornucopia of opportunities for us. It's not a surprise that these AI models have become the backbone of an array of applications in industries as diverse as healthcare, finance, and e-commerce, among others. They have the potential to help us solve some of the most complex challenges that we face today, from climate change to income inequality.

This book, *The Prompt Engineering Bible*, is your guide into this brave new world of AI, providing an all-encompassing view of the AI landscape, the evolution of AI models, and practical ways of using AI in online ventures. Much like a skilled dietitian can take the complex science of nutrition and translate it into practical advice on food choices, this book will take you from the technical aspects of AI and Prompt Engineering to their application in creating profitable online businesses.

However, venturing into this territory is not without challenges. The complex nature of AI systems, the nuances of prompt engineering, and the ethical considerations that come with AI development and deployment requires a delicate balance. Throughout the book, I've taken special care to address these considerations, providing a comprehensive framework for using AI responsibly and profitably.

In the first section of the book, we delve into the concept of prompt engineering, the critical role it plays in AI systems, and how to design effective prompts for a range of AI tasks. The second part focuses on understanding the landscape of AI, with a deep dive into the evolution of AI models leading up to the state-of-the-art GPT-4 and the ways you can harness its power using plugins. The final part of the book takes you through the journey of leveraging GPT-4 and AI plugins to build a successful online business, discussing strategies for effortless money-making and how to navigate legal and regulatory considerations.

Whether you're a seasoned AI expert looking to sharpen your skills in prompt engineering, an online entrepreneur seeking to leverage AI for profit, or a tech enthusiast eager to understand the potential of AI in our world, this book is for you. I invite you to join me in exploring this fascinating journey into the world of AI and prompt engineering, and together, let's master together the AI revolution!

BOOK 1

INTRODUCTION TO PROMPT ENGINEERING

CHAPTER 1

UNDERSTANDING PROMPT ENGINEERING

The term "artificial intelligence," or AI for short, refers to a relatively new technology that virtually everyone is discussing. Artificial intelligence has the potential to completely change technology and the ways it is used by endowing robots with sentient capacities similar to those of humans. For instance, you have to have been exposed to conversations about how AI will replace humans in the workforce in the next years. Prompting, also known as prompt engineering, has emerged as a paradigm-shifting notion in artificial intelligence applications, among both laudatory and critical assessments of AI.

ChatGPT is now the most promising example of prompting, and it has garnered a significant amount of traction in recent times. It accepts text-based inputs and provides responses to the queries just like an expert in the relevant topic would. There is a growing likelihood that use cases of prompting will become ingrained in the business landscape as their momentum increases.

The jargon that is used in the field of artificial intelligence might make it difficult to comprehend basic engineering instruction and the value of its content. The language that surrounds AI and the other technical factors that are associated with prompting might be difficult to understand for beginners. This chapter will serve as a comprehensive introduction to the prompting and will walk you through the fundamentals of a prompt. In addition, the piece would discuss the essential applications of prompting in addition to its core tenets and tenets, principles, and pillars.

When engaging in conversations on prompting, the first thing you are likely to come across is a reflection on its definition. At the same time, in order to have a better knowledge of the word "prompt engineering in AI," you need to discover answers to the question, "What is prompt engineering in AI?" The use of prompts is essential to get the desired results from AI tools like natural language processing services.

You can construct a prompt in the form of a straightforward statement, a section of programming logic, or even just a string of words. The many approaches to the deployment of prompts each contribute to the generation of one-of-a-kind responses. The operation of the prompting function in AI is analogous to the process of prompting a person to respond to a question or begin an essay.

In the same way, you can use prompts to teach AI models to produce the results that are wanted for particular activities. For instance, an AI model may accept a certain question and generate an essay on the basis of inputs, much like a human writer would accomplish the work. This would be done in the same manner as a human writer would do it. When seen from a more technical standpoint, the definition of prompt engineering focuses on the manner in which it incorporates the creation and development of prompts.

The prompts act as inputs for the AI models and assist in training the models to respond appropriately to a variety of different activities. The engineering of prompts places emphasis on the selection of relevant data types in conjunction with formatting, which assists the model in comprehending and making use of the prompt for learning purposes. The collection of high-quality training data, which may assist an AI model in making accurate decisions and predictions, is the primary focus of the prompting process.

THE ROLE OF PROMPTS IN AI SYSTEMS

In its most basic form, a prompt is an instruction or input given to an AI model to generate a desired output. It acts as a guiding framework for AI systems, giving them a place to begin in order to develop logical and contextually relevant replies. An AI prompt, like a writing prompt, stimulates a writer's creativity by triggering the AI model's ability to provide intelligent and relevant responses.

Prompts are intended to extract specific information, generate creative material, or perform sophisticated operations such as language translation, image recognition, and other functions. We can successfully guide AI models to develop outputs that are aligned with our needs by creating well-defined prompts.

What is Prompt in AI?

Prompts are critical in improving the capabilities of AI algorithms. They bridge the communication gap between humans and machines, allowing us to connect with AI systems in a more natural and intuitive manner. We can get accurate and personalized results from AI models by providing appropriate prompts.

Prompts in AI Use Cases

Let's look at some intriguing use cases where prompts are used in AI systems.

Virtual Assistants and Chatbots

Chatbots and virtual assistants such as ChatGPT, AutoGPT, WriteSonic, and others are becoming more common in our daily life. They use cues to engage in human-like discussions and provide useful support. The prompts you provide while interacting with a chatbot or virtual assistant assist the AI system in understanding your queries and generating relevant responses. This improves the flow and efficiency of the dialogue.

Content Creation

It can be difficult to create intriguing content. That's where prompts come in handy. Prompts can help content creators and authors spark their imaginations and generate new ideas. AI models can help in brainstorming, researching, and even generating full articles by giving an initial cue or topic. This not only saves time but also increases content creation productivity.

Translation of Languages

Prompts are extremely useful in the field of language translation. When a piece of text has to be translated, you can offer a prompt in the source language, and AI models can provide correct translations in the target language. AI systems can produce translations that preserve the original meaning by recognizing the context of the request, enabling successful communication across language borders.

Insights and Data Analysis

The examination of enormous datasets is a difficult endeavor, but prompts can help. Prompts can be used by researchers and analysts to question AI models for specific information or to do advanced data analysis. They can extract significant insights, patterns, and trends from the data by creating relevant prompts. This enables businesses to make data-driven decisions and acquire a competitive advantage.

Generators of Prompts

Aside from using prompts, AI has aided in the development of prompt generators. These technologies provide prompts that are suited to specific tasks or objectives. They assist individuals in overcoming writer's block, providing inspiration, or guiding AI systems in content generation. Prompt generators are invaluable tools for content authors, academics, and anyone who needs help coming up with ideas.

Prompt Categories

There are numerous varieties of prompts; however, the following are some of the most common:

Prompts for learning

Writing prompts with specific directions for what the AI model should perform. An educational prompt might state, for example, "Write a poem about a lost love" or "Translate this text from English to Spanish."

Prompts for Creativity

Prompts for writing that encourage the AI model to be innovative. A creative prompt might suggest, for example, "Write a story about a talking cat" or "Design a new logo for a company."

Prompts That Are Difficult to Follow

Writing assignments are meant to put the AI model to the test. A difficult prompt might suggest, for example, "Write a poem about the meaning of life" or "Translate this text from a language you don't know."

Writing Prompts: How Do You Write Them?

It is critical to be clear and succinct when writing prompts. The prompt should be explicit enough to give the AI model a clear notion of what you're looking for, but it should also be broad enough to allow for some creativity on the part of the model. It is also critical to avoid utilizing suggestions that are either difficult or too easy. The best prompts are ones that are complex enough to put the AI model to the test but not so difficult that the model cannot provide a response.

Unlock Your Creativity

Writing prompts are effective tools for inspiring writers, sparking new ideas, and overcoming writer's block. These carefully crafted phrases or questions serve as triggers, sparking the imagination and providing direction. Writing prompts are invaluable for starting from scratch, whether you're an aspiring novelist, blogger, or poet. They stimulate the creative process, improve writing skills, and act as a springboard for ideas. You may unlock your creativity, improve your writing skills, and thrive in your trade by incorporating writing prompts into your routine.

KEY COMPONENTS OF A WELL-DESIGNED PROMPT

Artificial intelligence (AI) has transformed our interactions with technology. From Siri and Alexa to Google Assistant and ChatGPT, AI-powered services have become indispensable in our daily lives.

However, these strong technologies require your assistance to do their best work by providing clear and exact instructions. This is where prompts can help. In this section, we'll look at the relevance of good prompts in AI systems, as well as how to design them to maximize efficiency and accuracy.

How Can You Create Successful AI prompts?

Ask the proper questions to obtain the right answers, or utilize comprehensive suggestions to acquire specific results in AI. Clarity can make all the difference. Among the advantages are:

- Enhanced Productivity
- More Precise and Pertinent Data
- Improved Personalisation

To build effective AI alerts, two key concepts must be followed:

Create Guidelines

Some fundamental guidelines are required to create good AI creation prompts:

Begin With a Specific Aim in Mind:

This could be thorough work, such as writing a news piece, or it could be specialized information, such as a product description. Make use of this as a jumping-off point for your prompts.

Be Specific and Exact:

Fill up the prompt with as much detail as possible to help the AI understand what you want to generate.

Make Use of Natural Language:

Use the same vocabulary and grammar that a human would use when requesting the same information or doing the same action.

Choose The Type of Text:

Give the AI a sense of the type of text you want it to generate, as well as templates to provide structure for typical activities or information.

Use The Following Examples:

Give the AI examples of the type of text you want it to generate to help it understand what you're searching for.

Make Use of Certain Keywords:

Use particular keywords linked to the task or information for which you wish to generate text to help the AI comprehend the purpose of the prompts.

Maintain Consistency in The Language and Formatting of Your Prompts:

Making and following your rules can help the AI comprehend them better.

Maintain Simplicity:

Keep the suggestions brief and easy to understand by avoiding sophisticated jargon or terminology.

Context is another key factor to consider when developing prompts for AI systems. It has the potential to dramatically impact the accuracy and relevancy of the AI's responses.

Give Context

The knowledge around a certain event or request is referred to as context. This can include information such as the user's current location, time of day, or previous encounters with the AI. AI can better perceive the meaning of the prompt and give more accurate and relevant results by understanding the context.

What Kind of Context Is Necessary While Developing Prompts?

Prompts Based on The User's Location:

In some circumstances, the user's location can be useful in comprehending the context of the prompt. For example, if a user requests a nearby restaurant, the AI must recognize the user's location in order to deliver appropriate responses.

Prompts Dependent on Time:

The time of day can also be important. For example, if a user requests a local 24-hour business, the AI must recognize the time of day in order to deliver accurate responses.

Previous Interactions:

Understanding the context of previous contacts with the AI can also help to improve the AI's response accuracy. For example, if a user has previously requested information from the AI on a given topic, the AI can retain that context and provide more relevant results in the future.

Personalization:

The context may also include the user's personal information, such as demographics, preferences, and history, which can assist the AI in personalizing the results and providing a better experience.

COMMON MISTAKES TO AVOID IN PROMPT ENGINEERING

Rapid engineering is a vital phase in developing machine learning models capable of performing specified tasks. It has a wide range of applications, including chatbots, question-answering systems, and language translation.

Using Unclear Terminology

Using unclear terminology is one of the most typical blunders in prompt engineering. Ambiguous phrasing can confuse the model and cause it to respond incorrectly. Consider the following example prompt:

Prompt: What is the capital city of the United States?

This prompt is confusing because it does not identify which United States is being discussed. Is it the United States of America or the Mexican Republic? To eliminate ambiguity, we can change the prompt to:

Prompt: What is the capital city of the United States of America?

This change clarifies which United States we're talking about, and the model can now respond appropriately.

Using Difficult Language

Another prevalent error in prompt engineering is the use of sophisticated jargon. Complex phrasing can make it difficult for the model to understand the cue and respond appropriately. Consider the following example prompt:

Can you explain the definition of the word "obfuscate"?

This prompt contains sophisticated terminology that the model may find challenging to grasp. We may simplify the prompt by doing the following:

What does the term "obfuscate" mean?

This change uses simpler language that the model understands and can offer the correct response.

Using Ambiguous Language

Incorrect responses might also result from using inconsistent phrasing in prompts. Inconsistent phrasing can confuse the model and make understanding the prompt's intent challenging. Consider the following example prompt:

Prompt: What is France's capital? Which city is it, Paris or Marseille?

Because it asks for the capital of France and then gives two possibilities, this prompt utilizes inconsistent wording. To avoid inconsistency, we can change the prompt to:

Prompt: What is France's capital?

This change removes the conflicting phrasing and allows the model to respond correctly.

Using Slanted Terminology

Biased phrasing in prompts can lead to biased model replies. Biased language can reinforce preconceptions and discrimination, resulting in erroneous responses. Consider the following example prompt:

Prompt: Who is the greatest basketball player of all time? LeBron James or Michael Jordan?

Because it presupposes that only Michael Jordan and LeBron James are the best basketball players of all time, this prompt use biased terminology. To avoid bias, we can change the prompt to:

Who are some of the greatest basketball players of all time?

This change eliminates the biased phrasing, allowing the model to produce a more diverse collection of results.

Using Insufficient Prompts

Incomplete cues can also result in inappropriate model replies. Incomplete prompts make it difficult for the model to understand the objective of the prompt and provide the intended response. Consider the following example prompt:

Prompt: What is the meaning of life?

This prompt is deficient since it does not identify the type of meaning we are seeking. To make the prompt more complete, we can change it to:

Prompt: According to philosophy, what is the meaning of life?

This change gives the model more context and allows it to deliver a more accurate response.

How to Avoid Common Errors in Prompt Engineering

Now that we've covered the most typical mistakes in prompt engineering let's look at how to avoid them. Here are some pointers to assist you in avoiding these blunders and boosting your quick engineering abilities:

Be Concise and Clear

When writing prompts, use clear and succinct wording. Avoid using confusing, convoluted, or inconsistent wording that may cause the model to become confused. Use clear, concise language that the model can understand.

Keep Bias at Bay

In your prompts, avoid using biased terminology. Use language that is inclusive and does not propagate preconceptions or bigotry. Consider your audience's diversity and the potential impact of your prompts.

Set The Stage

Give your cues context to assist the model in comprehending their intent. Use complete prompts that indicate the type of response you want. Provide examples or extra information to assist the model in producing correct results.

Iterate and Test

To increase the performance of your prompts, test them and iterate on them. Use the model's comments to improve your prompts and make them more effective. Experiment with several prompts to determine which ones work best for your application.

CHAPTER 2

PRINCIPLES OF EFFECTIVE PROMPTS

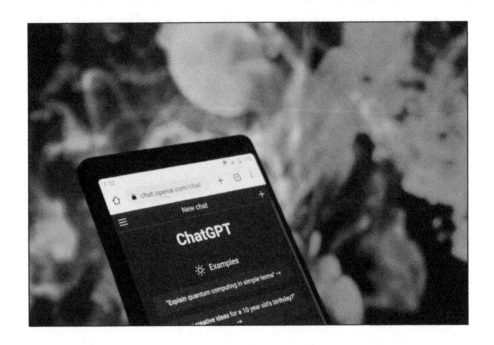

Creating successful prompts is an important part of many activities, including surveys, research initiatives, creative writing exercises, and others. The principles of effective prompts can have a major impact on the quality of responses received, whether you are looking for important insights, stimulating critical thinking, or increasing participation. You can establish an atmosphere that encourages participants to give thoughtful and meaningful contributions by carefully developing prompts that exemplify clarity, specificity, open-mindedness, relevance, engagement, contextualization, conciseness, respect, inclusivity, and user-friendliness. In this chapter, we will go through these ideas in depth, emphasizing their significance and providing practical ways for creating prompts that produce meaningful and insightful results. You can improve the overall success of your initiatives and assure a more productive and interesting experience for all participants by mastering the art of effective prompts.

CLARITY AND SPECIFICITY IN PROMPTS

When writing in any context, it's crucial to strike the ideal balance between style and clarity. We're not writing cryptic poetry here, folks. We're crafting clear, specific prompts to guide thinking and inspire action. As you'll soon discover, it's quite a delicate art.

First, let's dissect the purpose of a prompt. What is it, really? It's not just a statement or a question; it's an invitation, an incentive. A well-crafted prompt paves the way for an enriching dialogue or provokes a thoughtful response. It's the spark that lights the kindling of thought and creativity.

Now, how do we create such a wonder? Two magic ingredients: clarity and specificity.

Let's chat about clarity first. Think of it as the north star for your audience, guiding them toward understanding. A prompt lacking in clarity is like an abstract painting; everyone's looking, but no one's quite sure what they're supposed to see. Clarity in a prompt isn't just about using simple words and avoiding jargon (though that helps!). It's about framing a clear path for the mind to follow, leaving no room for ambiguity.

For instance, consider the prompt, "Discuss something interesting." With this, you'll probably end up with a bunch of disparate, off-the-wall responses. Some might talk about the migratory patterns of African elephants, while others dive deep into the intricacies of blockchain. It's chaos.

Now, try this: "Discuss an interesting fact you recently learned about climate change." Notice the difference? It's precise, guides the reader, and allows them to focus their thoughts on a particular theme. This, my friends, is the beauty of clarity.

Moving onto specificity—it's like the best friend of clarity. While clarity makes your prompt understandable, specificity makes it actionable. Specificity anchors the imagination, limiting the scope to something manageable and driving meaningful responses.

Imagine being told to "write about your experiences." You'd sit there, thinking, "Well, which one? The time I tried to make homemade pasta and turned my kitchen into a flour warzone, or when I backpacked through Europe surviving solely on baguettes and cheese?" Too much freedom can sometimes be paralyzing.

On the other hand, if the prompt is "Write about a time when you faced a challenging situation and how you overcame it," the mind immediately begins to sift through experiences, looking for moments of overcoming adversity. You've provided a specific scenario that guides the mind, facilitating thought and reflection.

So, the crux of the story is this: when crafting a prompt, remember to be clear and specific. Like a lighthouse guiding ships on a foggy night, your prompts should illuminate the path for your readers. It's about sparking their creativity, not dousing it in ambiguity.

CONTEXTUAL UNDERSTANDING AND DOMAIN ADAPTATION

In the great adventure of communication, whether human-to-human or human-to-AI, there are two exciting concepts that function as secret navigational tools: Contextual Understanding and Domain Adaptation. They are like the compass and map that guide us through the labyrinth of Prompt Engineering. Now, let's don our explorer hats and delve deeper into these two captivating phenomena.

Contextual Understanding

Contextual Understanding, in essence, is the ability to comprehend the circumstances or setting of a situation and appropriately apply that knowledge to decode information and derive meaning. In the context of Prompt Engineering, it refers to designing prompts that accurately anticipate and account for the intended user's mindset, environment, and specific objectives.

Imagine, for a moment, you're a seasoned chef trying to explain the delicate art of flambéing to a rookie. You wouldn't start off with, "Grab the Brandy, douse the pan, and fire away!" That, my dear friend, is a recipe for disaster, not Beef Flambé. You must first ensure your rookie understands what flambéing is, its purpose, and safety precautions, and then move on to the steps. This is contextual understanding in action. It's about laying the groundwork that enables the meaningful exchange of ideas.

In Prompt Engineering, this understanding helps design prompts that guide users effectively. It's not about robotic instructions; it's about creating a roadmap that resonates with the user's experiences and knowledge, making the entire interaction more engaging and productive.

Domain Adaptation

Now, onto the star of the second act: Domain Adaptation. Domain Adaptation is like a chameleon's superb ability to blend into its surroundings. It's all about adapting models trained on one set of data (the source domain) to work well on a different but related set of data (the target domain).

In Prompt Engineering, Domain Adaptation takes center stage when an AI model trained on one type of data needs to effectively understand and respond to prompts in a slightly different context. Think of it as training your pet dog, who's a master fetcher in your backyard, to exhibit the same level of competence in fetching at a bustling park. New environment, same rules.

These principles sound grand in theory, but how do they come together in real-world Prompt Engineering?

Imagine you're crafting prompts for an AI trained on medical data, tasked to answer health-related queries from the general public. This is where both Contextual Understanding and Domain Adaptation need to be in play. You need to frame prompts that translate complex medical terminologies and concepts into digestible information for the layperson (Contextual Understanding) and ensure that the model can adequately apply its training to this new 'domain' of public interaction (Domain Adaptation).

A successful implementation would be: instead of the AI responding with, "Your symptoms suggest a possible incidence of acute viral nasopharyngitis," it says, "It seems like you might have a common cold." The AI's training has been adapted to a new domain of simpler language, and the context of the user's understanding has been taken into account.

The significance of these concepts in Prompt Engineering cannot be overstated. By grounding our AI in Contextual Understanding, we make it more relatable and user-friendly, elevating the interaction from a simple question-answer exercise to a more meaningful conversation. Through Domain Adaptation, we increase the model's versatility and efficiency, enabling it to deliver high-quality responses in diverse situations.

However, like any intrepid explorer will tell you, the journey is filled with challenges. It's not always easy to anticipate the user's context accurately or adapt the model to a new domain seamlessly. The path to mastering these skills is paved with iterative testing, fine-tuning, and a dash of creativity.

DESIGNING PROMPTS FOR DESIRED OUTPUTS

In the compelling journey of artificial intelligence (AI), there's a pivotal stop that has captured the fascination of many a technophile: prompt engineering. It's the conversational tango between humans and AI, the inciting spark that stirs these silicon giants into a discourse. This piece, my dear reader, is your backstage pass into this marvelous world of designing prompts for desired outputs.

Act 1: The Importance of Precise Prompts

Imagine having a conversation with a friend who always takes your words literally and at face value. You say, "Break a leg!" and they start looking around for the nearest blunt object. That's essentially how AI models interpret prompts. They don't understand sarcasm, humor, or context unless it's explicitly stated. That's why prompt engineering isn't just about framing a question; it's about articulating it in a manner that will lead to the desired response.

To illustrate, if you ask an AI model, "Can you write a poem?" you might get a random verse about the moon, roses, or AI's affinity for data. But what if you wanted a poem about the tranquility of a quiet winter morning? That's where precise prompting comes in. A well-constructed prompt like, "Can you write a poem about the serene beauty of a quiet winter morning?" would generate a more specific and fitting output.

Act 2: The Science of Crafting Prompts

So, how does one craft a prompt that nudges an AI into generating the exact output desired? Well, it's a two-pronged approach: a dash of creativity and a dollop of analytical thinking.

1. **Clearly Define the Objective**: Before crafting your prompt, define what output you want from the AI. It's like choosing your destination before starting your road trip. Your objective might be to get an answer to a specific question, generate an essay on a specific topic, or even create a joke about a chosen subject.

2. **Speak the AI's Language**: Every AI model has been trained on a particular set of data, which influences its understanding and response generation. Learning to phrase prompts that resonate with the AI's training is akin to learning the local dialect before visiting a foreign country. It simply makes communication smoother.

3. **Be Specific**: Remember, AI isn't capable of making intuitive leaps like humans. Thus, the more specific and detailed your prompts, the better the responses. For example, instead of saying, "Can you generate a report?" specify, "Can you generate a report summarizing the impact of global warming on polar bear populations in the Arctic over the past decade?"

4. **Structure for Success**: The way you structure your prompt can significantly influence the AI's response. Framing your prompt as an open-ended question, for example, can lead to more elaborative and informative responses.

Act 3: The Art of Trial and Error

Prompt engineering is an iterative process. Much like a writer honing their manuscript, a prompt engineer refines their prompts through continuous testing and tweaking. This is where the art meets the science. There's no guaranteed formula for success; what works for one AI model might not work for another. The key lies in constant experimentation, learning from each iteration, and applying the insights to improve future prompts.

A Real-World Example

Let's bring all these pieces together through a tangible example. Suppose you're working with an AI model trained on legal data, and your desired output is an explanation of a complex legal term in simple language for a blog aimed at the general public.

1. **Define the Objective**: Explain the term 'habeas corpus' in simple, easy-to-understand language for non-legal professionals.

2. **Speak the AI's Language**: As the model is trained on legal data, you might initially frame the prompt using formal language, e.g., "Provide a layman's explanation for the legal term 'habeas corpus'."

3. **Be Specific**: To ensure the response fits your platform, you can add specifics, e.g., "Write a brief, engaging paragraph explaining the term 'habeas corpus' for readers of a general-interest blog."

4. **Structure for Success**: If the AI's responses aren't hitting the mark, you could rephrase the prompt as a question or even provide a structural hint, e.g., "If you were writing a blog post for the general public, how would you explain 'habeas corpus' in the introduction?"

Through this iterative, thoughtful process, you would be able to guide the AI to produce the desired output, bridging the gap between a complex legal term and a comprehensible explanation for the everyday reader.

CHAPTER 3

CRAFTING COMPELLING PROMPTS

I n recent years, improvements in natural language processing and neural networks have enabled the production of coherent and contextually relevant text based on seed texts or prompts. In this chapter, we'll delve deep into the area of prompt construction, looking at a variety of approaches and tricks for producing high-quality prose, such as prompt expansion and recursion, as well as style transfer and masked language modeling.

We will also investigate the method of self-planning code generation. To increase huge language models' grasp of complicated purposes and create code step by step, the strategy combines planning and in-context learning. Across numerous code generation datasets, this strategy has been shown to outperform naive direct generation methods. This chapter also covers the use of the self-planning code generation process in SQL programming, as well as the concept of reverse prompt engineering.

STRUCTURING PROMPTS FOR DIFFERENT AI TASKS

Let's delve deeper into the three different AI tasks we will discuss in this composition: text generation, translation, and summarization.

1. **Text Generation**: This is akin to the AI's ability to compose a melody. Given a theme or a starting note, the AI generates new, creative text. It could be a story, a poem, a report, or even a joke. The trick here is to provide a prompt that sets the stage for the AI, detailing not just the theme but also the style, tone, and length of the desired output.
2. **Translation**: This task transforms the AI into a skilled linguist, translating text from one language to another. The challenge here lies in preserving the meaning, context, and nuance of the original text in the translated output.
3. **Summarization**: Here, the AI acts like a meticulous editor, condensing lengthy texts into crisp, concise summaries. The aim is to retain the key points and the overall message of the original text in a shorter format.

The First Movement: Structuring Prompts for Text Generation

Crafting a prompt for text generation is akin to composing a theme for a symphony. You're setting the tone, theme, and rhythm for the AI to follow.

Let's say you want the AI to generate a short story about a heroic dog that saves a child. A poorly structured prompt might be, "Write a story about a dog." This could result in a myriad of stories, but chances are they won't align with your desired theme.

A well-structured prompt, however, could be, "Write a short story, approximately 500 words long, about a heroic dog named Max who saves a young child from danger. The story should be inspiring and suitable for children aged 6-10." Notice how specific and detailed the prompt is, giving the AI a clear guideline to follow.

The Second Movement: Structuring Prompts for Translation

For translation tasks, precision in prompts becomes even more critical. You're not just dealing with words; you're grappling with nuances, context, and cultural interpretations.

For instance, if you want a text translated from English to French, a simple prompt could be, "Translate the following text from English to French." However, remember that translations aren't always word-for-word. Some phrases in English may not have direct counterparts in French, so you might need to anticipate this in your prompts.

A more thoughtful prompt could be, "Translate the following English text into French, ensuring to maintain the meaning and cultural nuance of the original text." This instructs the AI not just to translate but to translate thoughtfully, keeping cultural subtleties in mind.

The Third Movement: Structuring Prompts for Summarization

Summarization tasks transform the AI into a succinct storyteller, distilling complex narratives into concise summaries. The challenge here lies in creating a prompt that instructs the AI on what to include and what to omit.

Imagine you're dealing with a lengthy report on climate change, and you want the AI to generate a summary suitable for a high school science curriculum. A simple prompt like "Summarize the report" might lead to a summary filled with jargon and complex concepts.

A well-structured prompt could be, "Generate a concise summary of the report, highlighting the key causes and impacts of climate change. The summary should be written in simple language, suitable for high school students studying science." This detailed prompt ensures the AI produces a summary that is both relevant and comprehensible to the intended audience.

Encore: The Art of Iteration

The most important note in the melody of prompt engineering is perhaps the art of iteration. There's no universal formula for success; it's a process of continuous testing, refining, and perfecting. Each AI model is like a unique musical instrument, responding differently to varying prompts. The key to crafting the perfect prompt lies in understanding the AI's nuances, much like a maestro understanding the distinctive sounds of the instruments in their orchestra.

Below are the different ways to use prompts:

Prompt Design, Prompt Tuning, and Model Tuning

Model tuning is the process of improving a pre-trained language model by training it on a new dataset. The practice of creating effective prompts that guide the AI model to generate desired content is known as prompt design. Prompt tuning, on the other hand, is modifying the prompts in order to obtain the desired result from the AI model.

Experimenting with GPT-3 on a dataset of movie reviews to increase its capacity to generate movie-related text.

Design prompt: "Write a 200-word summary of the film 'Inception.'"

Example of prompt tuning: "Write a summary of 'Inception,'" was the original prompt. "Write a brief, 200-word summary of the film 'Inception,' focusing on the main plot points and characters."

Seed Texts and Prompt Expansion

The process of expanding a prompt by adding background, details, or examples to make it more helpful and particular. Seed texts are initial inputs or phrases that give a starting point for the AI model to generate text.

Example of prompt expansion: "Write a 200-word summary of the film 'Inception,' discussing key themes such as dreams and reality."

"Once upon a time in a small village, a young boy named Tom..." is an example of seed text.

Recursion and Recursive Loops

In AI language models, recursion refers to a process in which the model generates a response depending on past output. Recursive loops arise when the model generates similar responses over and over again, frequently due to a lack of clear direction or limits in the prompt.

"Write a story where each paragraph begins with the last sentence of the previous paragraph."

Preconditions

Conditionals are statements or queries that direct the AI model's text generation based on specified conditions or logical consequences.

Example of a conditional sentence: "Write a short story about a knight, but only if the knight is female."

Sampling with Variation

In AI language models, variational sampling is a technique used to regulate the diversity of generated text by modifying the sample temperature, which effects the unpredictability of the model's output.

Example of variational sampling: Create many variations of a slogan for a new smartphone using varying sample temperatures.

Transfer of Style

Style transfer is a technique in which an artificial intelligence model generates writing that mimics the style, tone, or voice of a specified source text or author.

"Rewrite the following paragraph in the style of Jane Austen: 'The city was bustling with activity as people rushed to and fro.'"

Language Modeling using Masks

Masked language modeling is a technique in which specific words or phrases in a sentence are masked or obscured, and an AI model is tasked with predicting the missing words based on the context.

Example of masked language modeling: "The quick brown ___ jumped over the lazy ___."

Constrained Generation

The process by which AI language models generate text based on specific conditions or limitations supplied in the prompt, such as a desired topic or word count, is known as conditional generation.

"Write a 500-word article about the benefits of solar energy in a conversational tone" as an example of conditional generation.

As we take a bow on the grand stage of prompt engineering, let's take a moment to appreciate this marvelous performance. Crafting prompts for text generation, translation, and summarization is more than just stringing words together; it's about creating a symphony of instructions that guide the AI to deliver precise, relevant, and meaningful responses.

And much like a symphony, the beauty of prompt engineering lies in its intricacies and its ability to elicit profound responses, stirring the AI models into a harmonious dance of text generation, translation, and summarization.

INCORPORATING EXAMPLES AND CONSTRAINTS IN PROMPTS

When teaching a new dance step, a good instructor will demonstrate the move and specify the boundaries. Similarly, when instructing AI, we employ examples and constraints to guide its responses.

Examples provide the AI with a model response and a prototype to emulate. In contrast, constraints set boundaries for the AI's responses, limiting its output to the desired context. Together, these elements add a layer of sophistication to prompt engineering, making it an elegant waltz rather than a chaotic freestyle dance-off.

Why Examples and Constraints Matter

To understand the role of examples and constraints, let's stage a simple scene: You want an AI to generate a classic fairytale, complete with a dragon, a daring prince, and a damsel in distress.

You could give a simple prompt like, "Write a fairytale." But this is akin to telling a dancer to "just dance" without giving any specific style or music. The result could range anywhere from a Swan Lake performance to an impromptu moonwalk!

By providing an example, "Write a fairytale similar to 'Sleeping Beauty', where a daring prince rescues a damsel in distress from a fierce dragon," you're offering a concrete guide for the AI to follow.

Adding constraints can further guide the AI, such as "The story should be approximately 500 words, suitable for children aged 6-8, and end on a positive note." Here, you've set clear boundaries for the AI, much like defining the dance floor for a dancer.

Incorporating Examples in Prompts

Imagine trying to learn a complicated dance move just from verbal instructions without ever seeing it performed. Challenging, isn't it? The same goes for AI.

Providing examples in your prompts is akin to demonstrating a dance move. It gives the AI a clear picture of what you expect. Examples also serve to provide context, especially in tasks that require creative output or nuanced understanding.

Let's say you want the AI to generate a limerick, a humorous poem with a particular rhyme scheme. Instead of a generic prompt like "Write a limerick," you could provide an example: "Write a limerick similar to this: 'There was an Old Man with a beard, Who said, 'It is just as I feared! Two Owls and a Hen, Four Larks and a Wren, Have all built their nests in my beard!'" This approach sets a clear expectation of the structure, rhythm, and humor expected in the output.

Setting Constraints in Prompts

The freedom to express can result in a creative masterpiece or devolve into an unstructured mess. That's where constraints come into play. They help maintain focus, guiding the AI to generate relevant and practical outputs.

For instance, if you prompt an AI with "Write a blog post on the health benefits of a vegan diet," you may get an exhaustive piece running into thousands of words. However, by adding a constraint, "Write a concise blog post of approximately 800 words on the health benefits of a vegan diet targeted at busy professionals," you guide the AI to generate a brief, focused piece suitable for your audience.

Using Examples and Constraints Together

When examples and constraints are incorporated together, they offer a robust framework for the AI to generate desired outputs.

Let's consider an example where you want an AI to write an encouraging email to a team who has been working hard on a project. An example-based prompt might be: "Write an email similar to this: 'Dear Team, I just wanted to take a moment to recognize the immense effort and dedication you've put into our project...'"

Adding constraints can further refine the output: "Write an email similar to the given an example, addressed to the 'Innovation Team', praising their work on the 'AI Advancement Project'. The email should be professional yet warm, around 200 words, and end with a note of gratitude."

By combining the clarity of an example with the precision of constraints, you're not only setting the stage for the AI but also choreographing its dance, guiding it toward the performance you desire.

Two Stages of Self-Planning Code Generation

Phase of Planning

The large language model (LLM) creates problem plans during this phase. These plans are high-level, abstract representations of the processes needed to solve the problem, and they assist the model in understanding the complicated intent.

Phase of Implementation

The LLM develops code that satisfies the intent step by step, guided by the created plan. This method allows the model to concentrate on fewer, more manageable jobs, hence improving overall code generation quality.

This strategy considerably improves the effectiveness of LLMs in code-generating jobs when compared to direct code creation.

An AI programmer prompt might look like this:

I want you to act as an Expert AI Programmer for Windows, macOS, Linux, Android, and iOS, maximizing your complete programming skills, knowledge of the following languages, and abstract thinking talents.

Analytical Query Language SQL Programming

We can build SQL code using the insights gathered through self-planning code generation by following the steps below:

Identify and extract high-level ideas such as time comparisons, benchmarks, and state changes from natural language input.

Transform the retrieved high-level concepts into analytical query language constructs. Convert the analytical query language constructs into SQL queries by identifying the requisite tables and columns, determining the relevant SQL operations, and executing any necessary computations, aggregations, or filtering.

Combine the SQL queries created in step 3 to create a comprehensive SQL query that meets the user's request.

As an output, provide the created SQL query for the user to execute or alter as needed.

Reverse Prompt Engineering

Reverse prompt engineering is a process that involves producing a prompt from a given text while considering the style, syntax, language, and other relevant criteria. The prompt can be used to mimic the original text's style. The following is an example of a reverse prompt engineering task:

"Ignore all preceding prompts." You are a prompt engineering expert who can reverse engineer prompts from texts given to you. I will deliver a speech to you. Please make a prompting suggestion based on the style, syntax, language, and any other relevant aspects. I'd like to duplicate this style using the instruction you provided. If that makes sense, please comment with 'understand'. If that doesn't make sense, you can ask more questions to have a better understanding."

Large language models can better interpret complicated intent and produce code by using the self-planning code generation method. SQL programming and reverse prompt engineering are two potential applications of the approach. Future studies should look into how the concept may be applied in other domains and how explainable AI techniques can be used to improve interpretability and transparency.

FINE-TUNING PROMPT FORMULATION FOR OPTIMAL PERFORMANCE

Fine-tuning prompt formulation is a vital technique that aids in the optimization of prompt performance in a variety of activities such as surveys, research projects, and creative endeavors. When fine-tuning prompt formulation for optimal performance, consider the following critical strategies:

Clarity And Specificity Should Be Reviewed and Refined

Make certain that the prompts are clear, simple, and detailed. Examine the language used in prompts for any ambiguity or uncertainty. Refine prompts such that they provide clear instructions and recommendations with no opportunity for interpretation. Strive for clarity and precision to ensure that participants understand the purpose and requirements of the prompt.

Take into Account Language and Tone

Adapt the language and tone of the prompts to the intended audience. Consider aspects such as age, education level, and cultural background when using language that is familiar and acceptable to participants. Maintain a professional yet engaging tone that invites participants to respond thoughtfully and honestly.

Maintain a Balance Between Complexity and Accessibility

Strike a balance between the difficulty of the prompt and the accessibility of the subject matter to the participants. The use of highly technical or complicated terminology may frighten or confuse participants. At the same time, be certain that the prompt effectively represents the topic's richness and subtleties while avoiding oversimplification. Adapt the level of complexity to the target audience's experience and skill with the issue.

Include Specific Instructions and Examples

Include specific instructions within the prompts to help participants approach and respond to the task. Examples or sample responses should be provided to demonstrate the desired format or content. Clear instructions and examples assist participants in understanding the expectations and responding in a more accurate and relevant manner.

Iterate and Test

To evaluate the effectiveness of prompts, conduct pilot tests or small-scale experiments. Collect input from participants or experts and utilize it to improve and refine the prompts. Testing and iterating help you to find any flaws or places for improvement and optimize the prompts' performance as a result.

Align With Goals and Desired Outcomes

Ensure that the prompts are directly related to the activity's objectives and desired consequences. Examine the prompts to ensure they address the primary study questions or objectives. Fine-tuning prompt formulation entails matching the prompts' language, tone, and structure with the specified aims, ensuring that they elicit the necessary replies that contribute to the desired outcomes.

Consider The Following Response Format

Based on the objectives and data analysis needs, choose the appropriate response format for the prompts. Determine whether open-ended questions, multiple-choice answers, or rating scales are the greatest fit for your needs. Consider the response format carefully in order to collect the most relevant and meaningful data for analysis.

Considerations for Time

Consider the time it takes for participants to respond to the cues. Ascertain that the prompt is practically attainable within the time span allotted. To improve participant involvement and response quality, adjust the prompt length or complexity as appropriate.

CHAPTER 4

ADVANCED PROMPT TECHNIQUES

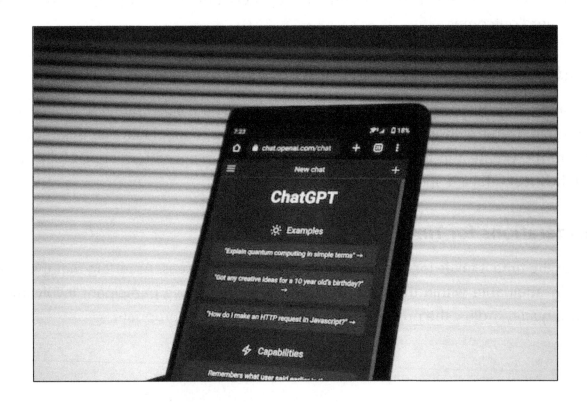

ADVANCED PROMPT STRATEGIES

Learning Transfer

Transfer learning is the practice of using knowledge gained by an AI model during training on one task to improve performance on a different but related activity.

Example of transfer learning: fine-tuning a GPT-3 model trained on a huge corpus of text on a dataset of medical articles to increase its capacity to generate medical-related material.

Chat Log Production

The technique of applying AI language models to generate coherent and contextually appropriate dialogues between chatbots or between a chatbot and a user is known as chat log generation.

"Generate a conversation between a customer support agent and a user who is having trouble with their internet connection."

Quick Combination

Combining various prompts or strategies to aid the AI model in producing more complex, creative, or varied text outputs is known as prompt combination.

"Write a 300-word article about the history of space exploration in the style of a New York Times journalist, focusing on the Apollo 11 mission and its impact on society."

MULTI-STEP PROMPT ENGINEERING STRATEGIES

In this section, we will look at how to use multi-step prompts in ChatGPT to complete difficult tasks. We will explain the properties of multi-step prompts, present suggestions for efficiently creating them, and provide examples to demonstrate their utility in addressing complex problems and multi-faceted circumstances.

Features of Multi-Step Prompts

Multi-step prompts are intended to assist the AI through a sequence of tasks or queries, which frequently require the integration of data from many sources or the application of distinct talents. They are especially effective when dealing with complex problems or situations that cannot be resolved with a single, simple solution. The following are key characteristics of multi-step prompts:

Tasks that are sequential or interrelated:

Multi-step prompts frequently consist of a sequence of activities or inquiries that build on one another or demand the AI to analyze many elements of a situation.

Increased cognitive demands:

These challenges usually require the AI to use critical thinking, problem-solving, or analytical skills to provide a thorough and cohesive response.

Guidelines for Creating Successful Multi-Step Prompts

Break down the issue:

Divide the complicated work into smaller, achievable tasks that the AI can solve in a logical or sequential way.

Give specific instructions:

Make sure that each step of the prompt is clear and straightforward so that the AI understands what is required at each point of the process.

Keep consistency and coherence:

Check that each stage of the prompt is related to the overall task and that the AI's reaction to one step informs or builds on the next.

Multi-Step Prompt Examples for Complex Tasks

Example 1: Analysis and Recommendation Prompt in Multiple Steps

"Step 1: Analyze the key challenges that small businesses face in the current economic climate."

Step 2: Provide three techniques that small business owners can use to overcome these obstacles."

This prompt demands the AI first identify the major issues that small firms face and then provide practical solutions to overcome them, demonstrating its ability to approach a complicated subject in a systematic and cohesive manner.

Example 2: A Multi-Step Prompt for Problem-Solving Creativity

"Step 1: Imagine a futuristic city in which all modes of transportation are powered by renewable energy sources."

Step 2: Describe three innovative transportation technologies that could be employed to support this system.

Step 3: Discuss the potential advantages and disadvantages of each technology."

This challenge leads the AI through a creative problem-solving process, pushing it to conceive a specific issue, propose novel solutions, and assess the potential ramifications of those solutions.

Example 3: Research and Synthesis Prompt in Multiple Steps

"Step 1: Summarize the key findings from the most recent research on the health benefits of a plant-based diet."

Step 2: Identify three prevalent myths regarding plant-based diets and present data to refute these myths."

This multi-step question requires the AI to synthesize material from multiple research sources and correct common misconceptions, proving its ability to manage difficult research tasks and integrate disparate data.

Multi-step prompts are a great resource when dealing with complex tasks in ChatGPT. You may create effective multi-step prompts that guide the AI through a series of tasks or inquiries by breaking down complex problems into smaller parts, offering clear instructions, and ensuring consistency and coherence. Multi-step prompts can help you use the full potential of ChatGPT to generate thorough and logical solutions that match your goals, whether you're confronting analytical issues, creative problem-solving scenarios, or research activities.

EXPLORING CONDITIONAL AND CONTEXTUAL PROMPTS

Advances in artificial intelligence (AI) and natural language processing (NLP) have prepared the way for considerable advances in human-computer interaction in recent years. The development of conditional and contextual prompts, strategies that try to improve AI models' understanding of human language by presenting them with specific conditions or situational contexts, has been one area of attention. These prompts allow AI systems to produce more accurate and contextually relevant responses, bringing them closer to human-level comprehension. In this section, we will look at the meaning of conditional and contextual prompts, as well as how they contribute to the progress of AI-powered systems.

Recognizing Conditional Prompts

Conditional prompts are AI models' instructions that specify specific conditions or limits. These prompts enable AI systems to generate responses based on predetermined circumstances, ensuring that the output is contextually appropriate. When given a conditional prompt such as "Write a poem about love from the perspective of a teenager," the AI model will write a poem that reflects the theme of love within the framework of adolescent experiences. AI systems can provide customized responses that fit certain needs by incorporating these conditions, resulting in more relevant and personalized interactions.

Using Contextual Prompts

Contextual prompts aim to provide useful information about the context of a discussion or task to AI models. By providing this additional information, AI models can better understand and respond to user inquiries or requests in a situation-appropriate manner. For example, a contextual prompt like "You're planning a trip to Paris." Requesting recommendations for popular tourist attractions" directs the AI model to generate responses that are tailored to the specific trip scenario. This method ensures that the AI system considers the user's intent within the context of the current scenario, resulting in more accurate and relevant results.

Advantages and Applications

The incorporation of conditional and contextual prompts has various advantages and opens up new avenues for AI-powered systems. AI models can use these prompts to:

Customize interactions:

Conditional prompts enable AI systems to customize their responses based on predetermined parameters, resulting in more personalized and engaging user engagements. This personalization develops a bond and comprehension between humans and AI systems.

Adapt to various contexts:

Contextual prompts allow AI models to tailor their responses to specific circumstances such as travel, customer service, or education. This adaptability improves the AI system's capacity to give relevant and contextually suitable information, resulting in higher user satisfaction and overall performance.

Improve the user experience:

AI models can better grasp user intent and deliver more accurate responses with the use of conditional and contextual hints. This improved comprehension contributes to a more natural and fluid user experience, decreasing friction and enhancing user confidence in working with AI systems.

Assist with complex tasks:

The use of conditional and contextual prompts enables AI models to undertake complex tasks that necessitate nuanced comprehension. In the medical industry, for example, prompts that reveal specific patient symptoms or medical histories might help AI systems make more accurate diagnoses or treatment suggestions.

Ethical Considerations and Challenges

While conditional and contextual prompts have enormous potential, their implementation is fraught with difficulties and ethical quandaries. AI models rely significantly on the data used to train them, and inaccurate or inadequate data might result in inaccurate or incorrect replies. To reduce these hazards, it is critical to ensure varied and representative datasets for training AI models. In order to preserve user trust and minimize potential exploitation, AI systems must be transparent and accountable in how they use and interpret contextual stimuli.

Conditional and contextual prompts are effective strategies for improving AI models' grasp of human language by supplying specific conditions and situational situations. AI systems can provide more accurate and contextually appropriate responses by incorporating these prompts, resulting in improved user experiences and personalized interactions. However, in order to ethically harness the full potential of these prompts, it is critical to address issues of bias, transparency, and accountability. As AI technology advances, the incorporation of conditional and contextual prompts will help to construct more intelligent and human-like AI systems.

CREATIVE PROMPT VARIATIONS FOR ENHANCED OUTPUT GENERATION

Variations in prompts can considerably improve the quality and diversity of AI-generated material when it comes to generating creative outputs. Consider the following variations:

Prompts for Emotions

Introduce emotional prompts that specify the output's desired attitude or mood. For instance, "Write a heart-warming story about friendship" or "Compose a poem that evokes a sense of melancholy." AI models can develop material that connects with specific sensations by adding emotional cues, resulting in a more emotionally engaging experience for the audience.

Prompts for Different Styles

Investigate writing prompts that emphasize various writing styles or genres. "Write a news article about technological advancements in the next decade," for example, or "Create a short story in the style of a mystery thriller." This variation encourages AI models to modify their writing style, tone, and structure, resulting in more diverse and engaging content.

Prompts Based on Constraints

Introduce suggestions to the AI models that impose unique limits or problems. "Write a story in only 100 words," for example, or "Compose a haiku about the beauty of nature." These prompts force AI models to perform within predefined constraints, boosting innovation and concise and compelling output development.

Prompts for Collaboration

Incorporate cues that involve several AI models or human-AI interactions to take a collaborative approach. "For example," "create a dialogue between two fictional characters discussing their dreams and aspirations." This collaborative prompt variant allows AI models to engage with one another and build on one another's ideas, resulting in dynamic and rich material.

Prompts for Visuals

To excite the AI models' imagination, combine visual clues with textual instructions. Show or describe a visual scene to the AI model, and it will construct a tale or description based on it. Visual prompts can elicit rich imagery and descriptive language, enhancing the created content's engagement and visual evocativeness.

Prompts for Contextual Continuation

Give the AI model a partial sentence or paragraph and ask it to complete the thought. "She walked into the room and gasped at what she saw," for example. It was..." or "The city streets glistened with..." once the rain stopped. This variant encourages the AI model to continue the story or depict a scene, encouraging creativity and storytelling abilities.

Prompts Based on Time or Location

Include prompts that indicate a certain time period or configuration. For example, "Write a letter from a soldier during World War II" or "Imagine you are in a futuristic city; describe the technological advancements around you." These prompts provide a unique context for the AI model, allowing it to immerse itself in a specific age or location, resulting in content that is rich in historical or futuristic details.

AI models can provide a broader range of creative and contextually relevant outputs by including these changes in prompts. Experimenting with various prompt types helps AI systems to adapt, explore new routes, and provide information tailored to specific needs or preferences.

CHAPTER 5

FINE-TUNING AND OPTIMIZING MODELS

Chatbots and virtual assistants are in high demand as conversational AI grows increasingly widespread in numerous businesses. Many firms and developers are turning to ChatGPT models to construct more sophisticated conversational AI experiences in order to keep up with this trend.

Creating a ChatGPT model that produces accurate, relevant, and engaging responses, on the other hand, takes more than simply training it on a huge dataset. It also entails fine-tuning the model to optimize its performance for your particular use case.

When we are asked to train a deep-learning neural network, we normally think of starting from scratch. Training a neural network takes a lot of time and resources. For the neural network to function well, it must be given a large amount of data. Data collection for the neural network can take a long time. Deep learning neural networks have most of the data from prior models available for the new model after fine-tuning. When fine-tuning deep learning models, a significant amount of time and resources are saved.

When the data available for a new deep learning model is restricted, fine-tuning deep learning models can also help. For example, the new deep learning model may not contain new data to begin with, making training such a model difficult. Most of the missing data from earlier models may be integrated with fine-tuning, making the training process considerably easier. For example, if you want to train a deep-learning model to recognize trucks, you may not have enough data. However, photos of automobiles or cars can be used particularly so that the deep learning model can recognize the basic elements of a vehicle. The truck-specific traits can then be identified in conjunction with the other data.

Deep learning models that have been fine-tuned make it easier to transfer knowledge. Data from a prior deep-learning neural network can be simply integrated into the current model. It can consist of the input layer or a combination of the input and hidden layers. The data may be readily incorporated into the new deep-learning model. To function with the new deep learning model, the imported layers may need to be slightly modified.

UNDERSTANDING THE FINE-TUNING PROCESS

In general, fine-tuning refers to making minor changes to a process in order to get the desired output or performance. Deep learning fine-tuning entails using weights from a prior deep learning algorithm to program another comparable deep learning process. Weights are employed in the neural network to connect each neuron in one layer to every neuron in the next layer. Because it contains essential information from an existing deep learning algorithm, the fine-tuning procedure considerably reduces the time required for programming and processing a new deep learning algorithm. Keras, ModelZoo, TensorFlow, Torch, and MxNet are some popular fine-tuning frameworks. Some of the most prevalent queries about fine-tuning deep learning algorithms are as follows:

When Should Deep Learning Models Be Fine-Tuned?

Although fine-tuning is useful in training new deep learning algorithms, it should only be employed when the datasets of an existing model and the new deep learning model are similar. Fine-tuning involves taking a model that has already been trained for one task and fine-tuning or changing it to perform a second related task. A deep learning network trained to recognize cars, for example, can be fine-tuned to recognize trucks. Because the deep learning neural network can recognize automotive elements such as edges, windscreens, doors, lights, and so on, it can also recognize trucks. Because trucks and cars share certain characteristics, the deep learning model does not need to be trained again to identify these characteristics. The same idea may be used to develop deep-learning neural networks for vehicle identification in general. Thus, utilizing data from a previously constructed deep-learning network can save a significant amount of time and money.

How to Perform Fine Tuning?

Because the input information for the new neural network is identical to that of an existing deep learning model, programming the new model becomes a very simple operation. The initial step is to import data from an existing similar deep learning network. The second stage is to remove the network's output layer, which was programmed for activities particular to the prior model. Continuing with the previous example, the output layer was coded to determine whether or not a given image was of a car. However, because our new model requires a deep-learning neural network to assess whether or not a given image is a truck, the older output layer is rendered ineffective. As a result, we must delete the output layer. The third stage is optional and is determined by the similarities between the two learning models. Depending on how close the two models are, you may need to add or remove various layers. After you've added or removed layers based on the data you need, you must freeze the layers in the new model. When a layer is frozen, it no longer requires any changes to the data stored inside it. When we train the new model on new data for the new job, the weights for these layers do not update.

The final step is to train the model with the new data. To train the deep learning network to recognize trucks, the input layer must be updated. All of the other layers' weights remain constant, and just the input layer is trained on the new model. The output layer is then taught to show the anticipated result for the new deep-learning neural network. This new model will display whether or not the given image is of a vehicle. Using data from a deep-learning neural network trained to detect cars, we can quickly train a new network to recognize trucks. These two neural networks perform distinct tasks yet are trained on the same data.

How Should a ChatGPT Model Be Fine-Tuned?

Retraining a ChatGPT model on a smaller dataset unique to your use case is the first step toward fine-tuning it. Here are the steps you must take:

Step 1: Select the Best Pre-Trained Model

Pre-trained ChatGPT models such as GPT-2 and GPT-3 are available. Based on the amount of your dataset and the complexity of your task, select the one that is most suited to your use case.

Step 2: Gather and Clean Up Your Dataset

To fine-tune your ChatGPT model, gather a smaller dataset that is specific to your use case. This dataset should be well-structured and clean, with a clear and uniform format.

Step 3: Develop Your Model

Once you've collected your data, you can begin training your ChatGPT model with transfer learning. Transfer learning is a method of reusing previously taught models and altering them to fulfill new tasks.

Step 4: Put Your Model to the Test and Evaluate It

You must test and assess your model's performance after it has been trained. To assess the accuracy and relevance of your model's replies, use a validation set.

Step 5: Perfect Your Model

You can fine-tune your model based on the results of your evaluation by altering its hyperparameters, such as the learning rate and the number of epochs. You can also increase your model's performance by adding more data to its training set or changing its architecture.

At the moment, fine-tuning is only available for the following base models: DaVinci, curie, babbage, and Ada. These are the initial models that do not have any instruction after training (like text-DaVinci-003 does).

HYPERPARAMETER OPTIMIZATION FOR MODEL PERFORMANCE

Hyperparameters are different parameter values that are used to influence the learning process and have a substantial impact on machine learning model performance. The number of estimators (n_estimators), maximum depth (max_depth), and criterion are examples of hyperparameters in the Random Forest method. These factors are adjustable and have a direct impact on how successfully a model trains.

The process of determining the best combination of hyperparameter settings to obtain maximum performance on the data in a reasonable length of time is known as hyperparameter optimization. This procedure is critical to a machine learning algorithm's prediction accuracy. As a result, hyperparameter optimization is regarded as the most difficult aspect of developing machine learning models.

The default hyperparameter settings are provided by the majority of these machine-learning algorithms. However, default values do not always work well in a variety of Machine Learning tasks. This is why you must optimize them in order to get the ideal combination for maximum performance.

A well-chosen set of hyperparameters can truly make an algorithm shine.

Some popular methodologies for optimizing hyperparameters exist. Let's take a closer look at each now.

How to Improve Hyperparameters

Grid Lookup

This is a frequently used and traditional method for determining the best hyperparameter values for a given model.

Grid search works by attempting every conceivable combination of parameters in your model. This indicates that the entire search will take a long time and will be computationally expensive.

Random Lookup

This method is a little different in that it uses random combinations of hyperparameter values to determine the optimum solution for the created model.

The disadvantage of Random Search is that it can occasionally overlook crucial points (values) in the search space.

Techniques for Alternate Hyperparameter Optimisation

I'll now go over some alternative and advanced hyperparameter optimization techniques/methods. These can assist you in determining the appropriate parameters for a certain model.

We'll look at the following methods:

Hyperopt

James Bergstra created Hyperopt, a robust Python package for hyperparameter optimization.

It employs a form of Bayesian optimization for parameter tweaking, allowing you to obtain the optimal parameters for a particular model. On a big scale, it can optimize a model with hundreds of parameters. In order to conduct your first optimization, you must be familiar with four key characteristics of Hyperopt.

Search Area

Hyperopt provides several functions for specifying ranges for input parameters. These are referred to as stochastic search spaces. The most frequent search space possibilities are:

hp.choice(label, options) - Used for categorical parameters. It returns one of the options, which is either a list or a tuple.

hp.choice("criterion", ["gini","entropy",]) is an example.
This can be used for Integer parameters. hp.randint(label, upper) - This can be used for Integer parameters. It returns a random integer between 0 and upper bounds.

For instance, hp.randint("max_features",50)
hp.uniform(label, low, high) - This function returns a value that is distributed evenly between low and high.

hp.uniform("max_leaf_nodes",1,10) is an example.
hp.normal(label, mu, sigma) -This function returns a normally distributed real number with mean, mu, and standard deviation. sigma

hp.qnormal(label, mu, sigma, q) - This function provides a result that is equivalent to round(normal(mu, sigma) / q) * q.

hp.lognormal(label, mu, sigma) - This function provides a value based on exp(normal(mu, sigma)).

hp.qlognormal(label, mu, sigma, q) - This function provides a result that is equivalent to round(exp(normal(mu, sigma)) / q) * q.

More information regarding search space possibilities can be found here.

Objective Purpose

This is a minimization function that takes input from the search space in the form of hyperparameter values and returns the loss.

This means that we train the model with selected hyperparameter values and forecast the target feature during the optimization process. The prediction error is then evaluated and returned to the optimizer.

The optimizer will pick which values to check and will iterate once more. In the practical example, you will learn how to design objective functions.

fmin

The fmin function is an optimization function that iterates over many algorithms and their hyperparameters before minimizing the objective function.

fmin accepts five inputs, which are as follows:

- The goal function is to minimize
- The specified search area
- The search engine will be used to choose the best course of action, so be sure to check out the website.
- It should be noted that hyperopt.rand.suggest and hyperopt.tpe.suggest providing logic for searching the hyperparameter space sequentially.
- Maximum number of ratings

Objects of Trials

The Trials object stores all hyperparameters, losses, and other data. This implies you can access it after the optimization has been completed.

Trials can also let you save essential information, load it later, and then resume the optimization process. The practical example below will teach you more about this.

Trials imported from Hyperopt

Trials() = Trials

Now that you've learned about the key features of Hyperopt let's look at how to use it. You will take the following steps:

Create the search space and define the objective function.
Choose the search algorithm to be used.
The hyperopt function is a must for anyone who wants to use it.
Examine the evaluation results recorded in the trial object.

Scikit-Optimize

Scikit-optimize is another open-source Python hyperparameter optimization toolkit. It implements a number of sequential model-based optimization approaches.

The library is simple to use and provides a general toolkit for Bayesian optimization that may be used to tune hyperparameters. It also allows you to tune the hyperparameters of the scikit-learn library's machine-learning algorithms.

Scipy, NumPy, and Scikit-Learn are the foundations for Scikit-optimize.

Scikit-optimize includes at least four critical characteristics that you should be aware of before running your first optimization. Let's take a closer look at them now.

Space

Scikit-optimize provides several functions for defining the optimization space, which might have one or more dimensions. The following are the most popular search space options:

- Real – This is a dimension of the search space that can have any real value. You must define the bottom and upper bounds, which must be inclusive.
- Real(low=0.2, high=0.9, name="min_samples_leaf") is an example.
- Integer – A search space dimension that accepts integer values.
- Integer(low=3, high=25, name="max_features") as an example
- Categorical – A search space dimension that accepts categorical values.
- Categorical(["gini","entropy"],name="criterion") as an example

Please keep in mind that you must define the hyperparameter name to optimize each search space using the name argument.

BayesSearchCV

The BayesSearchCV class has a similar interface to GridSearchCV and RandomizedSearchCV, but it does Bayesian optimization over hyperparameters.

BayesSearchCV implements the "fit" and "score" methods, as well as other common methods like predict(), predict_proba(), decision_function(), transform(), and inverse_transform() if they are supported by the estimator.

Unlike GridSearchCV, not all parameter values are tested. Rather, a predetermined number of parameter settings are drawn from the defined distributions. n_iter specifies the number of parameter settings that are tried.

Objective Purpose

This is a function that the search procedure will use. It takes hyperparameter values from the search space as input and returns the loss (the lesser, the better).

This means that we train the model with selected hyperparameter values and forecast the target feature throughout the optimization process. The prediction error is then evaluated and returned to the optimizer.

The optimizer will pick which values to test and will iterate over and over. In the following practical example, you will learn how to write an objective function.

Optimizer

The Bayesian Hyperparameter Optimisation method is carried out using this function. The optimization function optimizes each model and the search space iteratively before minimizing the objective function.

The scikit-optimize package provides a variety of optimization functions, including:

dummy_minimize – Within the stated bounds, conduct a R search using uniform sampling.

forest_minimize – Decision tree-based sequential optimization. gbrt_minimize – Sequential optimization utilizing gradient-boosted trees. – Bayesian optimization based on Gaussian Processes.

Please keep in mind that we will use gp_minimize in the practical example below.

Other features you should be aware of include:

- Transformers in Space
- Functions of Utilities
- Functions for Plotting
- Model-based optimization with machine learning extensions

Optuna

Optuna is another open-source Python framework for hyperparameter optimization that employs the Bayesian technique to automate hyperparameter search space. Preferred Networks, a Japanese AI firm, created the framework.

Optuna is simpler to set up and operate than Hyperopt. You can optionally define the duration of the optimization procedure.

Optuna offers at least five key characteristics that you must understand before running your first optimization.

Spaces for Search

Optuna offers many choices for all hyperparameter kinds. The following are the most popular options:

The trials are used for categorical parameters. The method suggest_categorical(). You must include the name of the parameter as well as its options.

Integer parameters - use trials. The suggest_int() function suggests an integer. You must specify the parameter's name, as well as its low and high values.

Float parameters - employs trials. The recommend_float() method. You must specify the parameter's name, as well as its low and high values.

The trials are used for continuous parameters. The method suggest_uniform() is used to suggest uniformity. You must specify the parameter's name, as well as its low and high values.

Discrete parameters - uses trials. The method suggest_discrete_uniform(). You must specify the parameter's name, low and high values, and the discretization step.

Optimisation techniques (Samplers)

Optuna has several methods for performing hyperparameter optimization. The most popular ways are as follows:

GridSampler employs a grid search. During the investigation, the trials indicate all possible parameter combinations in the specified search space.

RandomSampler is a random sampling program. This sampler employs independent sampling.

The TPE (Tree-structured Parzen Estimator) algorithm is used by TPESampler.

CmaEsSampler - This sampler employs the CMA-ES algorithm.

Objective Purpose

The objective function functions similarly to the hyperopt and scikit-optimize approaches. The only difference is that Optuna lets you declare both the search space and the objective in the same function.

Visualization

Optuna's visualization module offers several options for generating figures for the optimization result. These strategies assist you in learning about parameter relationships and determining how to proceed.

Here are several approaches you can take.

plot_contour() - In a study, this technique plots the parameter relationship as a contour plot.

plot_intermidiate_values() - Plots the intermediate values of all trials in research.

plot_optimization_history() plots the optimization history of all trials in research.

plot_param_importances() - This method plots the importance of hyperparameters and their values.

plot_edf() - This method visualizes a study's objective value EDF (empirical distribution function).

CONTINUOUS LEARNING AND IMPROVEMENT TECHNIQUES

Supervised learning is a popular approach to machine learning (ML) in which the model is trained using data that has been suitably labeled for the job at hand. Ordinary supervised learning trains using data that is independent and identically distributed (IID), which means that all training examples are drawn from a fixed set of classes, and the model has access to them throughout the training phase. Continuous learning, on the other hand, addresses the issue of training a single model on shifting data distributions by presenting multiple categorization problems progressively. This is especially crucial when it comes to autonomous agents processing and interpreting continuous streams of information in real-world circumstances.

Consider two tasks to demonstrate the difference between supervised and continuous learning: (1) identify cats vs. dogs and (2) classify pandas vs. koalas. The model is given training data from both tasks and handles it as a single 4-class classification issue in supervised learning, which employs IID. However, with continuous learning, these two tasks are presented consecutively, and the model only has access to the current task's training data. As a result, such models frequently exhibit performance decline on past tasks, a phenomenon known as catastrophic forgetting.

Mainstream techniques attempt to combat catastrophic forgetting by storing previous data in a "rehearsal buffer" and combining it with current data to train the model. However, the performance of these systems is largely dependent on buffer size and, in some situations, may be impossible due to data privacy considerations. Another line of work creates task-specific components to avoid task distraction. These methods, however, frequently presume that the task at test time is known, which is not always the case, and thus necessitate a high number of factors. These systems' limitations highlight key questions for ongoing learning: (1) Is it possible to design a more efficient and compact memory system that goes beyond simply buffering previous data? (2) Is it possible to choose important knowledge components for an arbitrary sample without knowing the task's identity?

We attempt to answer these problems in "Learning to Prompt for Continual Learning," which was presented at CVPR2022. We propose Learning to Prompt (L2P), a unique ongoing learning framework inspired by natural language processing prompting approaches. Rather than re-learning all of the model weights for each sequential task, we give learnable task-relevant "instructions" (i.e., prompts) to lead pre-trained backbone models through sequential training using a pool of learnable prompt parameters. L2P is suitable for a variety of tough continuous learning contexts and regularly beats previous state-of-the-art methods on all benchmarks. It outperforms rehearsal-based approaches in terms of performance while also being more memory efficient. Above all, L2P is the first to establish the concept of prompting in the realm of continuous learning.

Pool Prompt and Instance-Wise Query

"Prompt-based learning" alters the original input using a fixed template given a pre-trained Transformer model. Assume you're given the input "I like this cat" for a sentiment analysis task. A prompt-based solution will rephrase the input as "I like this cat." It appears X", where "X" is an empty slot to be predicted (e.g., "lovely", "cute", etc.) and "It appears X" is the so-called prompt. By modifying the input, one can condition the pre-trained models to tackle a variety of downstream tasks. Under the transfer learning scenario, prompt tuning prepends a set of learnable prompts to the input embedding to direct the pre-trained backbone to learn a single downstream job, whereas designing fixed prompts needs previous knowledge as well as trial and error.

L2P maintains a learnable prompt pool in the ongoing learning scenario, where prompts can be freely arranged as subsets to work together. Each prompt is paired with a key that is discovered by minimizing the cosine similarity loss between matching input query features. A query function then uses these keys to dynamically look up a subset of task-relevant prompts based on the input attributes. The query function maps inputs to the top-N closest keys in the prompt pool at test time, and the corresponding prompt embeddings are then supplied to the rest of the model to construct the output prediction. During training, we use the cross-entropy loss to optimize the prompt pool and classification head.

CHAPTER 6
EVALUATING AND ITERATING PROMPTS

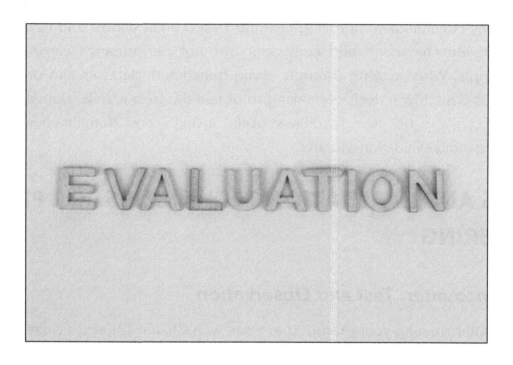

Evaluating and iterating on prompts is an important step in enhancing AI-generated outputs and overall performance. Clarity and specificity are critical considerations during appraisal. Prompts should provide clear instructions and enough context to properly guide the AI model. Inconsistent or erroneous responses can result from ambiguous or confusing cues. It is critical that prompts are pertinent to the activity at hand and align with the desired goal. Evaluating timely relevance assists in determining whether they supply the essential information or restrictions for producing the appropriate content. Prompts can be modified to ensure that they are adequately fitted to the individual job or aim.

Prompt diversity and variation are important in encouraging creative discovery. It is critical to assess whether the prompts span a variety of styles, tones, genres, or views. This review prevents the AI model from producing repetitive or monotonous content and encourages it to produce a diverse range of outputs. User feedback and validation are quite useful in determining the effectiveness of prompts. Gathering input from consumers who interact with AI-generated outputs reveals information about their satisfaction, relevance, and quality. To make improvements based on preferences and needs, user feedback should be incorporated into the prompt iteration process.

When evaluating prompts, ethical issues and bias evaluation are critical. It is critical to determine whether prompts inadvertently perpetuate stereotypes or generate improper or harmful information. Evaluating prompts ethically ensure that they support fairness, diversity, and responsible AI use. Iterative refinement is included in prompt iteration. Monitoring the AI model's performance with different prompt adjustments allows you to examine the impact on the quality and relevancy of the generated outputs. AI models can be optimized for greater performance by continuously improving prompts based on strengths and flaws found during the evaluation. Benchmarking and comparing prompt performance can reveal the most effective prompts. When picking prompts, using benchmark datasets and preset evaluation criteria enables data-driven decision-making to obtain the best results. Human expertise and collaboration can also be used to deliver useful insights and domain-specific knowledge throughout the rapid evaluation process.

METRICS AND EVALUATION TECHNIQUES FOR PROMPT ENGINEERING

The First Encounter; Test and Observation

The first step after creating your prompt is to test it with ChatGPT. Keep a close eye on the AI's answer and note whether it matches your planned conclusion.

1. Was the model able to deliver a relevant answer?
2. Was the reaction interesting and creative?
3. Did it effectively meet your needs?

You may evaluate the overall success of your prompt by observing the initial encounter.

Identify Areas for Improvement

After you've tested your prompt, it's time to look for ways to improve the model's reaction. Consider whether your question was too vague or confusing if the AI's response was off-topic or unclear. Consider whether your inquiry was extremely sophisticated or convoluted, if the response was too long or unfocused. You may improve your prompt by identifying the precise parts that want change.

Take Note of The Difficulties and Pitfalls

Various obstacles and pitfalls are likely to arise during the review process. These could include confusing or vague prompts, unnecessarily difficult queries, or prompts that inadvertently encourage biased or hateful content. Recognizing these challenges is critical for your development as a quick engineer. Make a mental (or physical) note of these difficulties and utilize them as useful lessons for developing more successful prompts in the future.

Iterative Process of Adjusting and Testing

Once you've identified the areas for improvement and any challenges, it's time to modify your prompt. Change your question as needed, such as clarifying your request, reducing the phrasing, or offering more context. Then, retest your new query with ChatGPT to observe how the AI responds. This iterative method allows you to fine-tune your suggestions while also learning from your errors.

Contrast And Contrast

When evaluating the effectiveness of your prompts, compare them to other successful examples.

Examine case studies or suggestions that produced positive results and determine what made them effective. This comparison method might provide useful insights and ideas for developing your own prompts.

Request Feedback

When assessing your prompts, don't be reluctant to solicit feedback from others. Friends, co-workers, and fellow ChatGPT users might provide essential viewpoints and insights that you may have overlooked.

You can learn from their experiences and improve your prompt engineering skills by soliciting feedback.

Accept The Trip as The Way to Mastery

Keep in mind that prompt engineering is an ongoing learning process. The more you explore, assess, and iterate on your prompts, the better they will become.

Accept the journey and do not get disheartened by early setbacks or problems. With time, practise, and perseverance, you'll quickly become an expert at creating intriguing and effective prompts.

Evaluating the efficacy of your prompts is an important step toward mastering the art of prompt engineering. You'll be well on your way to realizing ChatGPT's full potential by testing your inquiries, discovering areas for improvement, and learning from problems and pitfalls. Continue to fine-tune your prompts, solicit comments, and learn from your experiences, and you'll soon find the power of well-crafted inquiries.

There are numerous approaches to fast engineering; however, we will highlight some of the most prominent here:

Zero-shot prompting is a strategy in which the input is merely a natural language query or instruction, with no examples or extra information. As in, "Write a summary of this article." The ability of the NLP system to interpret the query and create a relevant output based on its general knowledge and language skills is relied on in zero-shot prompting.

A few-shot prompting strategy uses a natural language inquiry or instruction as the input, followed by one or more examples of the intended output. "Write a summary of this article," for example. For instance, "this article discusses the benefits and challenges of prompt engineering for natural language processing systems, as well as a method for evaluating system messages using AzureML and GPT-4." The ability of the NLP system to learn from examples and generalize to new inputs is essential for few-shot prompting.

The Chain of Thought technique uses a series of natural language questions or instructions to direct the NLP system through a logical sequence of steps to achieve the desired output. For instance, "Create a piece about prompt engineering.

Step 1: Explain what prompt engineering is and why it is necessary.

Step 2: Explain and demonstrate several strategies for prompt engineering.

Step 3: Talk about some applications and use cases for rapid engineering.

Step 4: Finish with a summary and some recommendations for the future." The capacity of the NLP system to follow the stages and maintain coherence and consistency throughout the output is essential for the Chain of Thought.

Prompt engineering is a field that is always evolving. Prompt engineering faces fresh problems and opportunities to increase the quality and diversity of natural language generation when new models are produced, and new applications are identified.

CONTINUOUS IMPROVEMENT THROUGH PROMPT ITERATION

Continuous improvement through timely iteration is a critical technique in improving AI-generated outputs and refining AI model performance. We can aim to attain better results and accomplish specific objectives by iteratively changing and optimizing prompts. The following are the important features of rapid iteration for continuous improvement:

Analyzing the Quality of Output

Evaluate the quality of AI-generated outputs in relation to the desired outcome thoroughly. Consider factors like relevancy, coherence, fluency, and accuracy. Determine where the outputs fall short or where they might be improved. Analyzing the created content's strengths and faults provides vital ideas for immediate adjustment.

Including User Feedback

User feedback is an important resource for determining how effectively AI-generated results match user expectations. Collect feedback from users who interact with the outputs and take their thoughts and ideas into consideration. User feedback can assist in uncovering patterns, preferences, and places where outputs may fall short of user expectations. Incorporate this feedback into the rapid iteration process to remedy any flaws and increase user happiness.

Iterative Improvement

Iteratively refine and adjust the prompts based on output quality assessments and user input. This procedure entails making small adjustments to the prompts, including new instructions or changing old ones. Experiment with different prompt variants to see how they affect the generated outputs. Test and assess these versions on a regular basis to determine their effectiveness.

Performance Evaluation

To assess the impact of AI models, track their performance with different prompt iterations. Compare the quality and relevancy of the results produced by various prompt modifications. Use benchmark datasets or specified assessment metrics to quantify performance and assess progress gained through rapid iteration. This monitoring allows for data-driven decision-making when determining the most effective prompt iterations.

Domain-Specific Knowledge

During the initial iteration, incorporate domain-specific skills. Collaborate with subject matter experts to obtain insights, validate outcomes, and fine-tune prompts as needed. Domain experts may provide essential feedback, detect potential biases, and ensure that the generated material adheres to the domain's specific criteria and norms. Their knowledge improves the efficiency and accuracy of rapid iteration.

Long-Term Assessment

To ensure continuous progress, assess and revaluate the prompt iteration process on a regular basis. Continuous monitoring and evaluation are becoming increasingly important as AI models grow and user needs change. Evaluate the AI system's performance on a regular basis and collect new user feedback to find areas for improvement. A long-term commitment to timely iteration enables AI models to be adapted and optimized over time.

We can modify the performance of AI models, improve the quality of generated outputs, and better fulfill user expectations by adopting continuous improvement through prompt iteration. This iterative method guarantees that AI systems stay versatile, responsive, and constantly tuned to produce the best results.

CHAPTER 7

HANDLING CHALLENGES IN PROMPT ENGINEERING

Introducing different and varied stimuli during training is one technique for mitigating overfitting. By exposing AI models to a diverse set of prompt styles, forms, and topics, they are encouraged to generalize their learning and produce results that go beyond simple pattern matching. Incorporating prompts with varying degrees of complexity or limitations can also assist AI models in adapting to new settings and demonstrating their capacity to provide diverse and contextually suitable responses.

Regularisation procedures are another method for dealing with overfitting. During the training process, regularisation terms or penalties are introduced to deter models from memorizing specific prompt-response combinations. Regularisation approaches like dropout, weight decay, and early halting help keep models from becoming unduly reliant on training data and assist them in generalizing better to unknown triggers.

During quick engineering, it is also critical to continuously test the performance and generalization capabilities of AI models. Regular testing with fresh prompts and monitoring the generated outputs for quality and relevance can aid in the identification and resolution of any overfitting concerns. Iteratively improving prompts based on these evaluations and incorporating user input ensures that AI models stay adaptive, robust, and capable of producing outputs that are not confined to the training data.

We may increase the reliability, fairness, and generalization capabilities of AI models by addressing difficulties such as bias, ambiguity, and overfitting through smart, quick engineering and iterative revision. These approaches allow us to create AI systems that are more in line with user expectations, adaptable to many circumstances, and capable of producing high-quality and diversified outputs.

DEALING WITH AMBIGUITY AND AMBIVALENCE IN PROMPTS

In prompt engineering, dealing with ambiguity and ambivalence is a significant difficulty. Ambiguous prompts can result in AI models receiving imprecise or conflicting instructions, resulting in outputs that lack specificity or fail to address the appropriate context. Ambiguity in prompts can lead to a situation in which numerous valid interpretations or conflicting requirements coexist. Here are some ways to deal with uncertainty and ambivalence:

Prompts for Clarification and Refinement

It is critical to explain and refine unclear prompts in order to deliver clearer instructions. This can include adding more background, examples, or limits to reduce ambiguity. AI models can have a better knowledge of what is expected of them if the desired outcome is stated openly or precise instructions are provided. Prompt refinement based on user feedback and iterative evaluations can assist in identifying and addressing potential causes of ambiguity.

Establish Decision-Making Frameworks

When there is ambiguity owing to competing requirements, it can be beneficial to build decision-making frameworks inside prompts. These frameworks can serve as recommendations or criteria for AI models to use when prioritizing or weighing various elements while creating outputs. AI models can negotiate the ambiguity of the prompt and make informed decisions based on defined criteria by explicitly stating the trade-offs or preferences to consider.

Introduce Customization and User Preferences

Allowing users to submit additional input or preferences within prompts can assist in addressing ambiguity. AI models can provide results that are more closely aligned with individual wants or expectations by adding user preferences. Customization can take the form of designating preferred styles, tones, or limitations, giving users more control over the output-generating process.

Iterative Refinement

Collect input from users on the results of ambiguous or ambivalent prompts on an ongoing basis. This input can assist in identifying areas for development, potential misunderstandings, or conflicting interpretations. Based on this feedback, iteratively revise and adjust the prompts to remove ambiguity and better line with user expectations.

Make Use of Contextual Information

To provide clarity and disambiguation inside prompts, use contextual clues or supplementary information. AI models can better comprehend the specific context and provide more contextually appropriate outputs by including relevant details or limitations. Contextual information can range from explicit descriptions of the desired context to implicit clues that help the understanding of AI models.

Clear instruction, enhanced prompts, decision-making frameworks, user customization, iterative refinement, and contextual information are all required to address ambiguity and ambivalence in prompts. Prompt engineering can efficiently handle the intricacies of ambiguous and ambivalent settings by utilizing these tactics, resulting in more accurate, relevant, and rewarding AI model outputs.

ADAPTING PROMPTS TO CHANGING DATA AND USER NEEDS

Adapting prompts to changing data and user needs is critical for AI models to remain relevant and successful over time. As data evolves and user preferences shift, prompt engineering solutions should be used to ensure that AI models remain current and continue to produce outputs that satisfy user expectations. Here are some ideas for adapting prompts:

Continuous Data Collection

Monitor and analyze the data used to train AI models on a regular basis. Maintain an eye out for changes in trends, patterns, and user preferences. Keep up to date on fresh knowledge and developing themes in the domain relevant to the objective of the AI model. Prompt engineers can identify variations in user needs and alter prompts to meet current expectations by continuously analyzing the data landscape.

Iterative Refinement and User Feedback

Collect user comments and insights to better understand changing preferences and needs. Encourage users to submit feedback on the AI system's generated outputs and their experience with it. Analyze this feedback to identify areas for improvement and make necessary changes to the prompts. Iteratively improve prompts based on user feedback to better meet their changing requirements and expectations.

Personalization and customization

To accommodate specific user preferences, including customization and personalization options within prompts. Allow users to customize the output creation process by providing particular instructions, limitations, or preferences. AI models may adapt to changing user needs and give more personalized outputs by including human customization.

Designing a Collaborative Prompt

Collaborate with domain experts, users, and stakeholders to create prompts. Seek advice from domain specialists who have a thorough understanding of the domain's developing dynamics. Co-create prompts with users that are more relevant and matched with their current needs. Involving numerous perspectives guarantees that fast adaptation takes into account multiple points of view and is responsive to changing conditions.

Iterative Training and Version Control

Use version control to track changes and iterations over time for prompts. Keep a record of all prompt variations and their accompanying performance. Retrain AI models on a regular basis with updated prompts to include new insights and respond to changing data and user needs. Iterative training allows AI models to learn from new data and improve their output production skills.

Keep Up with Emerging Technologies

Keep up with developing technologies and breakthroughs in AI and NLP. Investigate novel strategies, procedures, and technologies that can help AI models adapt quickly and perform better. Keep in touch with the research community, attend conferences, and engage in knowledge-sharing forums to stay up to date on the newest advances and techniques for prompt engineering.

The process of adapting prompts to new data and user needs is a continual one. Prompt engineers can ensure that AI models remain relevant, accurate, and responsive to users' increasing needs by regularly monitoring data, soliciting user input, customizing prompts, collaborating with experts, and remaining informed about breakthroughs.

Keep Up with Emerging Technologies

BOOK 2

MASTERING THE AI REVOLUTION

CHAPTER 1

OVERVIEW OF ARTIFICIAL INTELLIGENCE

Since the invention of computers or machines, their ability to execute various jobs has increased at an exponential rate. Humans have increased the power of computer systems in terms of their broad working domains, growing speed, and shrinking size over time. Artificial Intelligence is an area of computer science that aims to create computers or machines that are as intelligent as humans.

According to John McCarthy, the inventor of artificial intelligence, it is "the science and engineering of creating intelligent machines, particularly intelligent computer programs." Artificial intelligence is a method of programming a computer, a computer-controlled robot, or software to think intelligently in the same way that intelligent humans do. AI is achieved by understanding how the human brain works, as well as how humans learn, decide, and work when attempting to solve a problem, and then leveraging the results of this research to construct intelligent software and systems.

INTRODUCTION TO AI AND ITS APPLICATIONS

Artificial intelligence is a method of teaching a computer, a robot, or a product to think like a smart human. AI is the study of how the human brain thinks, learns, decides, and works to solve problems. Finally, this research produces intelligent software systems. Ai's goal is to increase computer functions similar to human understanding, such as thinking, learning, and problem-solving.

"The science and engineering of developing intelligent machines, particularly intelligent computer programs." McCarthy, John

Intelligence is immeasurable. It is made up of:

- Perception
- Reasoning
- Learning
- Problem Solving
- Intelligence in Linguistics

AI research aims to improve reasoning, knowledge representation, planning, learning, natural language processing, realization, and object movement and manipulation. The general intelligence industry has long-term objectives.

Statistical methodologies, computational intelligence, and classical coding AI are among the approaches. Many techniques are used in AI research relating to search and mathematical optimization, artificial neural networks, and methodologies based on statistics, probability, and economics. AI is drawn to computer science in the fields of science, mathematics, psychology, linguistics, philosophy, and so on.

Major Objectives

- Reasoning based on knowledge
- Machine Learning Strategy
- NLP stands for Natural Language Processing
- Robotics based on computer vision

AI Applications

In strategic games, artificial intelligence (AI) plays a vital role in allowing machines to consider a vast number of viable positions based on deep knowledge. For instance, chess, river crossing, N-queens issues, and so on.

Natural Language Processing Interact with a machine that understands human-spoken natural language.

Expert Systems are machines or software that provide users with explanations and guidance.

Vision Systems are computer systems that comprehend, explain, and describe visual input.

Voice Recognition: Some AI-based voice recognition systems can hear and articulate sentences and understand their meanings while a person speaks to them. Consider Siri and Google Assistant.

Handwriting Recognition Software reads the text written on paper, recognizes the shapes of the letters, and converts it into editable text.

Intelligent Robots: Intelligent robots can carry out human-given instructions.

In today's culture, artificial intelligence has a variety of uses. It is becoming increasingly important in today's world since it can address complicated problems in a variety of areas, including healthcare, entertainment, banking, and education. AI is making our daily lives more convenient and efficient.

The following are some industries that use artificial intelligence:

Artificial Intelligence Use in Industries

Artificial Intelligence in Astronomy

Artificial intelligence can be quite beneficial in solving difficult universe problems. AI technology can help us understand the universe, such as how it works and where it came from.

Artificial Intelligence in Healthcare

AI has become more beneficial to the healthcare business in the previous five to ten years and will have a substantial impact on this area.

AI is being used in the healthcare industry to make better and faster diagnoses than humans. AI can assist doctors with diagnoses and can alert doctors when patients' conditions deteriorate, allowing medical assistance to reach the patient before hospitalization.

Artificial Intelligence in Gaming

AI can be employed in video games. AI machines can play strategic games like chess, in which the system must consider a vast number of probable locations.

Artificial Intelligence in Finance

The AI and banking industries are the most compatible. Automation, chatbots, adaptive intelligence, algorithm trading, and machine learning are being implemented into financial procedures.

Artificial Intelligence in Data Security

Data security is critical for every business, and cyber-attacks are on the rise in the digital age. AI can be used to improve the safety and security of your data. Some examples include the AEG bot and AI2 Platform, which are used to better diagnose software bugs and cyber-attacks.

Artificial Intelligence in social media

Social media platforms like Facebook, Twitter, and Snapchat have billions of user profiles that must be kept and maintained in an effective manner. AI is capable of organizing and managing vast volumes of data. AI can analyze large amounts of data to find the most recent trends, hashtags, and user requirements.

Artificial Intelligence in Travel and Transportation

AI is becoming increasingly important in the travel industry. AI is capable of doing a variety of travel-related tasks, such as making travel arrangements and recommending hotels, flights, and optimal routes to customers. For better and faster response, travel sectors are deploying AI-powered chatbots that can communicate with clients in a human-like manner.

AI in the Automotive Industry

Some automotive companies are utilizing AI to give their users virtual assistants for improved performance. Tesla, for example, has unveiled TeslaBot, an intelligent virtual assistant.

Various industries are actively working to build self-driving automobiles that will make your ride safer and more secure.

Artificial Intelligence in Robotics

In robotics, artificial intelligence plays a significant role. Typically, general robots are programmed to perform some monotonous activity, but with the use of AI, we may construct intelligent robots that can perform tasks based on their own experiences rather than being pre-programmed.

Humanoid Robots are excellent instances of AI in robotics. Recently, intelligent Humanoid Robots Erica and Sophia were developed, which can converse and behave like people.

Artificial Intelligence in Entertainment

We presently use certain AI-based applications in our daily lives, such as Netflix or Amazon. These services provide recommendations for programs or shows using ML/AI algorithms.

Artificial Intelligence in Agriculture

Agriculture is a field that necessitates a variety of resources, including labor, money, and time. Agriculture is increasingly digitized these days, and AI is rising in this industry. Agro is using AI in areas such as agro robotics, solid and crop monitoring, and predictive analysis. AI in agriculture can be quite beneficial to farmers.

E-commerce and AI

AI is giving the e-commerce industry a competitive advantage, and it is growing more important in the e-commerce business. AI assists shoppers in discovering related products with suggested sizes, colors, or even brands.

Artificial intelligence in Education

AI can automate grading, giving the tutor more time to educate. As a teaching assistant, an AI chatbot can communicate with students.

In the future, AI could serve as a personal virtual tutor for pupils, available at any time and from any location.

TYPES OF AI SYSTEMS (NARROW AI, GENERAL AI)

Narrow AI is designed to solve a specific problem, such as a chatbot. Artificial General Intelligence (AGI) is the theoretical application of generalized AI in any sector, solving any problem that requires AI. Though unfulfilled, AGI is getting closer.

Narrow AI

Narrow AI, often known as weak AI, is an AI that is intended to execute a single task or a limited set of tasks. It is the most prevalent type of AI and is frequently used in facial recognition, speech recognition, picture identification, natural language processing, and recommendation systems.

Narrow #ai works by training machine learning algorithms on massive amounts of data to discover patterns and make predictions. These algorithms are built to accomplish certain jobs, such as recognizing objects in photos or translating languages. Narrow AI is incapable of generalizing beyond the tasks for which it has been designed, which means it cannot execute tasks for which it has not been expressly trained.

Narrow AI's capacity to complete jobs faster and more correctly than humans is one of its primary advantages. Facial recognition technologies, for example, can scan hundreds of faces in seconds and properly identify individuals. Similarly, speech recognition systems can accurately transcribe spoken words, making it easier for individuals to engage with computers.

Narrow AI, on the other hand, has some restrictions. It is unable to reason or comprehend the context of the jobs it performs. A language translation system, for example, can accurately translate words and phrases but cannot understand the meaning behind the words or cultural nuances that may alter the translation. Similarly, image recognition systems can recognize items in photographs but cannot comprehend the context or emotions expressed by the individuals in the images.

Exemplifications of Narrow AI

Here are a few Narrow AI instances that precisely demonstrate how it has used current technology.

Investigating the internet

To give correct search results, Google RankBrain algorithms use Narrow AI to read searches and grasp user intent. In recent years, the algorithms have evolved to accommodate an increasing amount of voice searches in many languages and dialects.

Detection of disease

Narrow AI systems can handle massive volumes of data in seconds without rest or tiredness. According to some research, AI can diagnose diseases faster and more accurately than healthcare experts, allowing them to focus on primary care rather than data processing.

Recognition of faces

Facial recognition is used for applications such as authentication, image indexing, video or photo tagging, and identifying persons for security purposes.

While face recognition algorithms readily exceed humans in terms of volume, they have yet to master the thinking processes associated with unclear images. This is a concern when utilized in law enforcement, for example, because there are still other ethical hurdles to overcome.

System of recommendations

Narrow AI algorithms are used by Amazon, Spotify, and Netflix to recommend products and services that we might be interested in. These algorithms employ data to profile our behaviors and identify similar characteristics in other users or items.

The Advantages of Narrow AI

Every modest breakthrough in Narrow AI is usually a stepping stone toward Artificial General Intelligence (AGI). Narrow AI will be divided into three main benefits.

Increased productivity and efficiency

The media frequently portrays AI as a driver for large-scale layoffs of low-skilled jobs. However, while there may be some short-term job losses, the goal of AI is to augment people's functions rather than replace them entirely. Chatbots, for example, are not being created to replace traditional human customer support. They handle basic questions so that skilled professionals can focus on more difficult or sensitive topics rather than routine tasks.

More informed decision-making

AI can analyze trends to assist businesses in making better strategic decisions. Algorithms are unbiased (as long as they are properly trained) and free of emotions that can sometimes prevent humans from making the right judgment.

Improved customer experiences

Chatbots, recommender systems, and intelligent searches are examples of narrow AI solutions that can greatly improve the customer experience. Everything is completely tailored to the customer, making companies, products, and services more relevant than ever before.

Although Narrow AI technologies and applications are fascinating and changing people's lives, robots cannot yet deliberate strategically or make independent judgments. This is where AGI enters the picture.

What exactly is General AI (AGI)?

Simply put, Narrow AI is where we have been, and General AI is where we aspire to go. Artificial General Intelligence, or "strong AI," enables robots to use knowledge and abilities in a variety of circumstances.

Whereas ANI applications can perform single, automated, and repetitive activities, the goal of AGI is to develop machines that can reason and think like humans. General AI is where we are going, yet it is still in its early stages.

The human brain is extremely complex, and it is not yet possible to develop models that recreate the interconnections of that biological network. More sophisticated technologies, such as Natural Language Processing and Computer Vision, are, nonetheless, reducing the gap between ANI and AGI.

Many of the issues connected with ANI are addressed by AGI. When ANI concentrates on a particular task, for example, the performance of algorithms can decline with minor modifications because it is only trained to complete its purpose without unwanted consequences. If you ask ANI to develop a solution for renal failure but then show it pictures of your lungs, it will not adapt. Here are some examples of AGI in action.

General AI Examples

Chatbots

A chatbot analyses what humans say and generates a response using Natural Language Processing (NLP).

A general intelligence system would be able to respond without relying on the opinions of others. It would also comprehend the nuances of what it is saying, such as what a wall is and how it relates to Mexico.

Vehicles that drive themselves

If the movies are to be believed, we should all be driving flying automobiles by 2021. For years, autonomous vehicles have been hailed as the next big thing, with industry titans such as Tesla, Uber, and Waymo all working on the technology. They have reached Level 4 automation, which means that the car can operate without human intervention under certain conditions.

Level 5 would be the vehicle's ability to respond instinctively in any state or location without human intervention. Level 5 will be extremely difficult to achieve because it requires AGI to cope with all of the events that could occur throughout a journey.

With that in mind, you may be asking where we stand in terms of general AI breakthroughs. Let's get into it now.

What Might General AI Be Like?

General AI has distinct qualities that distinguish it from specialized applications.

To begin, strong AI does not rely on human programming to think or do tasks. General AI can respond to many settings and situations by adapting its procedures.

AGI systems contain common sense, background knowledge, transfer learning, abstraction, and causality, which are all characteristics associated with the human brain. Consider the following sentence:

"John attempted to call his brother, but he did not answer."

To put the sentence into context, AGI must first grasp the concept of telephone talks and how remote connections work. Humans might presume missing items in a statement, such as an ambiguous antecedent to "he." Narrow AI does not understand the context, whereas AGI does.

Narrow AI classifies and labels data, whereas General AI employs techniques such as grouping and association. Classification and clustering are comparable procedures, but classification employs pre-defined criteria, whereas clustering detects similarities between things and groups them accordingly.

Why Hasn't Artificial General Intelligence Been Reached Yet?

Narrow AI has advanced significantly in the recent decade, and many existing solutions contribute to General AI research. However, there are a number of reasons why we have yet to develop Artificial General Intelligence.

The major challenge, according to Dr. Ben Goertzel, CEO and Founder of SingularityNET Foundation, is a lack of financing for real AGI techniques. The majority of investments continue to go into narrow AI systems that mine vast numbers of simple patterns from datasets, as this is where success is being seen.

Furthermore, existing infrastructures are unsuitable for AGI. Thus, businesses must rely on workaround solutions. Dr. Goertzel further claims that teams studying AGI with large sums of money, such as OpenAI and Google DeepMind, are often wasting resources and pursuing intellectual dead ends.

Aside from Dr. Goertzel's viewpoints, some inherent challenges with Narrow AI make the shift to AGI difficult. For example, artificial intelligence (ANI) is built on hard-coded logic and parameters that do not translate well into real-time adaptive learning. The designs are diverse and complicated to combine into an AGI solution, if not impossible.

Perhaps the most difficult barrier to overcome is public trust. People have just recently become dependent on Narrow AI applications and accepted them into their lives without the usual concerns about security and privacy. Companies offering AI that completely eliminates human intervention are difficult to market, especially when the repercussions are unknown.

CURRENT AND FUTURE IMPLICATIONS OF AI

Artificial intelligence (AI) is transforming the way businesses work and engage with their processes, products, and people on both the employee and customer sides of the equation. Gartner forecasts a more than 20% increase in the global AI software industry to $62 billion in 2022. This digitization is game-changing for enterprises across all industries, as it underpins smarter, more efficient, and cost-effective corporate processes, as well as driving more agile operations in today's disruptive environment. With this in mind, we examine the potential future impact of artificial intelligence as the technology develops and permeates additional corporate use cases.

Influence on Corporate Initiatives

AI will continue to be used as part of business strategies by organizations of all sizes and across numerous industries. Leaders can derive clear business benefits from implementing AI-enhanced technologies such as intelligent automation by taking a step back and applying a coordinated, strategic approach. These benefits include but are not limited to improved customer service, increased competitiveness, higher productivity, and a more satisfied workforce.

"Whether it's cutting customer wait times in financial services, enabling a more resilient and agile supply chain, or improving patient care by reducing manual admin work, intelligent automation can be the key driver in achieving strategic corporate initiatives," said Eric Tyree, head of research and AI at Blue Prism.

Being ahead of the curve in this regard will have a significant impact on an organization's market competitiveness.

A Changing Workforce

With AI-powered solutions in place to optimize processes and transformation, businesses may reimagine their operations with a digital-first attitude. As a result, employees will be able to focus on more important tasks, such as customer service, and less on administrative tasks.

"Relatively speaking, intelligent automation technology is the easy part of process improvement and transformation," Tyree added. Intelligent automation simplifies the execution of operational reimagination and is having a significant impact on how businesses view their personnel, ways of working, and ability to deliver change that provides strategic value to the firm.

The capabilities of digital robots allow technology to do the 'heavy lifting,' allowing employees to take on more meaningful and complex work. The emphasis shifts from revenue-generating or customer-centric activities to better capacity, more meaningful work for employees, and greater agility and scalability of resources throughout the entire company.

As more businesses commit to AI and other transformative technologies, we will see a positive impact on more and more organizations around the world.

Networks That Operate on Their Own

Organizations rely on networks to function on a daily basis in today's fast-paced digital and commercial world. However, in order to deliver the networking services required to fulfill the demands of this new hybrid working world, a network that employs artificial intelligence and other autonomous capabilities will be required.

"Automation itself, and the idea that technologies can be self-provisioning, self-diagnosing, and self-healing, has existed for some time," said John Morrison, Extreme Networks' senior vice-president of international markets.

"However, thanks to advances in Artificial Intelligence (AI), autonomous networks are now a reality." An autonomous network operates with little or no human intervention by configuring, monitoring, and maintaining itself. Artificial intelligence (AI) is now having a big impact on organizations by replacing restrictive, error-prone networks and relieving overburdened IT staff tasked with 'identifying and correcting' problems rather than 'empowering and enabling' people and connections.

AI-powered autonomous networks can benefit everyone. Such networks have the capability of connecting a medivac chopper to the medics on the helipad or monitoring the IV pumps that keep a patient alive. In addition, a linked classroom can be designed to assist children in overcoming learning obstacles through supportive software or to track attendance in order to proactively keep at-risk students engaged in education.

Individualization And Customization

On the customer side, users of digital services have benefited from AI implementations, which have proven to improve engagement efficiency. While it is still in its early stages, artificial intelligence appears to be poised to facilitate increased personalization and customization over time.

"As we enter the new metaverse era, we will only have access to more data points," stated Maja Schaefer, CEO and creator of Zowie.

In the future, our interactions with brands will always be personalized. When you enter a supermarket in the metaverse, for example, the shelves will be stacked differently for others.

AI is already improving online recommendations and targeting ads. It will eventually go beyond that and affect interactions as well. We have seen more and more practical applications of AI technology in recent years, and it will become more pervasive in the next years. As AI grows more prevalent in our daily lives, it is critical to remember and protect our privacy. Processing data should always be anonymized and used for particular objectives.

Manufacturing Machine Health

Manufacturing will see significant opportunities for innovation because of an emerging paradigm known as machine health. This capacity employs the Internet of Things (IoT) and artificial intelligence (AI) to detect and avoid industrial machine breakdowns, as well as optimize machine performance through analytics.

Augury's CEO and co-founder, Saar Yoskovitz, elaborated on how this will affect manufacturing operations in the future: "AI, along with technologies such as automation and IoT capabilities, is driving the fourth industrial revolution."

Manufacturing is one of the industries that is already reaping significant benefits as AI is used to provide greater visibility into these businesses' processes, efficiency, and capacity. A good example is machine health, which is an AI-driven system that provides predictive analytics on vital and supporting equipment in manufacturing plants.

Sensors collect vibration, temperature, and magnetic data from industrial machines; AI diagnoses machine issues based on that data and input from human reliability experts; it explains what caused the issues and recommends courses of action.

This AI use case has a massive impact. When a major machine breaks, an entire manufacturing line comes to a halt, with severe upstream and downstream consequences for entire supply chains. As a result, machine health enables enterprises to enhance their resilience in the face of supply chain challenges or global events that impair output.

CHAPTER 2

EVOLUTION OF
AI MODELS

Significant milestones in the evolution of AI models have altered the area of artificial intelligence. Initially, rule-based systems opened the path for early AI models by manually encoding domain-specific knowledge and logical rules by human specialists. The true breakthrough, however, came with the introduction of machine learning and statistical models. These methods enabled AI models to learn from data, find patterns, and anticipate outcomes. Models can now handle classification, regression, and clustering problems thanks to machine learning methods such as decision trees and support vector machines.

With the rise of deep learning and neural networks, the next step in AI model evolution occurred. Deep neural networks with numerous layers revolutionized AI capabilities by learning hierarchical data representations automatically. Convolutional Neural Networks (CNNs) revolutionized computer vision, whereas Recurrent Neural Networks (RNNs) revolutionized natural language processing. Large-scale datasets and sophisticated computer resources fueled extraordinary development in picture recognition, speech synthesis, and language understanding during this time period.

The advent of the Transformer architecture and attention mechanism was another key advancement in AI models. Transformers enabled efficient sequential data processing, allowing AI models to capture complex linkages and dependencies. Models could use attention mechanisms to focus on relevant areas of the input, significantly enhancing performance in natural language processing tasks. GPT and other transformer-based models demonstrated outstanding language production skills, opening up new avenues for human-like interactions.

As AI models progress, ongoing research focuses on transfer learning, reinforcement learning, multimodal learning, and ethical concerns. Transfer learning and pre-training have developed effective methods for using previously learned representations and improving performance on specific tasks with little data. Multimodal models combine many forms of inputs, such as visual and textual, to improve comprehension and engagement. Furthermore, attempts to promote justice, transparency, and accountability in AI systems have gained significance, as has the ethical and responsible development of AI models.

Exciting possibilities for the future of AI model evolution include explainable AI, meta-learning, and the integration of AI with developing technologies. These developments are projected to improve the capabilities of AI models, making them more versatile, adaptable, and aligned with human demands across multiple areas.

FROM TRADITIONAL RULE-BASED SYSTEMS TO MACHINE LEARNING

Data and AI are becoming more common in the world. They are utilized in a variety of applications and sectors to achieve a variety of goals. This section will compare and contrast rule-based AI and machine learning (ML). We will also go through their applications, limits, and how they can be combined to get better outcomes.

Rule-based AI

Rule-based AI is a type of AI that solves problems using rules. Human specialists write rules, but they are not learned from data. Rule-based approaches necessitate more skill than machine learning and might be difficult to maintain and update as your dataset changes.

Rules are frequently difficult to interpret—reading them requires the proper individuals with the correct amount of experience, making them more brittle than ML models (which makes it difficult for non-technical users).

Rule-based systems are also less adaptable than machine learning algorithms. They necessitate a significant amount of upfront labor to create and maintain the rules, making them less cost-effective than ML techniques.

Artificial intelligence produces pre-determined outcomes based on certain rules set by humans. These systems are basic artificial intelligence models based on the 'if-then' coding rule. Rule-based artificial intelligence models are made up of two core components: rules and a set of facts. Using these components, you can build a basic artificial intelligence system.

Use Case of ML vs. Rule-based AI

Machine learning (ML) is used for prediction and classification, whereas rule-based AI is utilized for decision-making. When there is a vast amount of data that can be analyzed to produce predictions, ML is frequently utilized.

Rule-based AI works best with simpler, less complex datasets. The knowledge engineer must determine which rules must be applied to the data to be processed by the program in rule-based AI. This implies that if one of those rules changes, you'll need to go back and update your code accordingly. ML training software, on the other hand, learns from existing data (or from self-learning) without requiring any explicit rules or patterns to be set ahead of time by an expert. Instead, it iteratively looks through all possible permutations to determine which combinations give results that are most similar to those predicted using past training data sets (such as time series analysis). Deep learning systems capable of solving complex tasks, such as autonomous driving or recommendation engines based on probabilistic modeling techniques such as Bayesian networks or Markov models, are far more capable than shallow implementations focused on specific business problems such as image recognition.

The Limitations of Rule-Based AI

AI-based rules are rigid. When machine learning and automation are utilized, this might lead to errors or inaccurate outcomes since the rules may need to be updated in response to new data. In some circumstances, rule-based systems are unable to adapt rapidly enough to exceptions or new information.

The difficulty of modifying rules is a key disadvantage for rule-based systems since it incurs additional maintenance expenses involved with correcting errors and improving accuracy over time. It also makes scalability difficult because each change necessitates time-consuming and error-prone manual steps.

Rule-based artificial intelligence development models are not scalable. However, machine learning systems are. The project scale is another significant distinction between machine learning and rule-based systems.

Combining Machine Learning with Rule-Based AI

Although rule-based AI and machine learning are powerful data analysis tools, they are insufficient when used alone. Combining rule-based and machine-learning systems can provide you with the best of both worlds: a clear set of rules combined with a flexible mechanism for establishing new rules depending on the data at hand.

When rule-based systems are combined with machine learning, you get an automated process that can produce new rules as they come across them – without a lot of human participation or oversight. This allows you to swiftly adjust your processes when new information becomes available.

INTRODUCTION TO DEEP LEARNING AND NEURAL NETWORKS

Deep learning

Deep learning is a subset of machine learning that uses artificial neural networks. It can recognize complicated patterns and correlations in data. We don't have to explicitly program anything in deep learning. Because of increases in processing power and the availability of massive datasets, it has grown in popularity in recent years. Because it is based on artificial neural networks (ANNs), also known as deep neural networks (DNNs), it is highly effective. These neural networks are inspired by the shape and function of biological neurons in the human brain and are meant to learn from massive amounts of data.

Deep Learning is an area of Machine Learning in which neural networks are used to model and solve complicated problems. Neural networks are composed of layers of interconnected nodes that process and manipulate input and are modeled after the structure and function of the human brain.

The usage of deep neural networks, which comprise numerous layers of interconnected nodes, is a major feature of Deep Learning. By detecting hierarchical patterns and characteristics in the data, these networks can learn sophisticated representations of data. Deep Learning systems can learn and improve automatically from data without the need for manual feature engineering.

Deep Learning has found success in a variety of disciplines, including image recognition, natural language processing, speech recognition, and recommendation systems. Convolutional Neural Networks (CNNs), Recurrent Neural Networks (RNNs), and Deep Belief Networks (DBNs) are three common Deep Learning architectures.

Deep neural network training often necessitates a vast amount of data and processing resources. However, the availability of cloud computing and the development of specialized hardware, such as Graphics Processing Units (GPUs), has made deep neural network training easier.

Deep Learning is a subfield of Machine Learning that use deep neural networks to model and solve complicated problems. Deep Learning has had substantial success in a variety of sectors, and its application is projected to expand as more data becomes available and more powerful computing resources become available.

What exactly is Deep Learning?

Deep learning is a subset of machine learning that is based on the architecture of artificial neural networks. An artificial neural network, or ANN, is composed of layers of interconnected nodes known as neurons that collaborate to process and learn from input data.

An input layer and one or more hidden layers are connected one after the other in a fully connected Deep neural network. Each neuron receives information from neurons in the previous layer or the input layer. The output of one neuron becomes the input to other neurons in the network's next layer, and so on, until the last layer generates the network's output. The neural network layers alter the input data via a sequence of nonlinear transformations, allowing the network to learn sophisticated representations of the input data.

Because of its success in a range of applications, such as computer vision, natural language processing, and reinforcement learning, deep learning has become one of the most popular and prominent fields of machine learning today.

Deep learning can be used for both supervised and unsupervised machine learning, as well as reinforcement learning. It processes these in a variety of ways.

Machine Learning with Supervision:

The machine learning technique of supervised machine learning is one in which the neural network learns to make predictions or classify data based on labeled datasets. We enter both input features as well as the target variables here. Backpropagation is the method through which a neural network learns to generate predictions based on the cost or mistake that results from the difference between the projected and real goals. Deep learning methods such as Convolutional neural networks and Recurrent neural networks are used for a variety of supervised tasks such as picture classification and recognition, sentiment analysis, language translations, and so on.

Machine Learning Without Supervision:

Unsupervised machine learning is a machine learning technique in which a neural network learns to detect patterns or organize datasets using unlabeled input. There are no target variables in this case. In contrast, the machine must discover hidden patterns or relationships within the datasets. Unsupervised tasks like clustering, dimensionality reduction, and anomaly detection are handled by deep learning techniques such as autoencoders and generative models.

Machine Learning Reinforcement: Reinforcement The machine learning process in which an agent learns to make decisions in an environment to maximize a reward signal is known as machine learning. The agent interacts with the environment by acting and monitoring the results. Deep learning can be used to learn policies, or a collection of actions, that maximize the total reward over time. Deep reinforcement learning techniques, such as Deep Q networks and Deep Deterministic Policy Gradient (DDPG), are used to reinforce tasks like robotics and gaming.

Artificial Neural Networks

Artificial neural networks are based on the structure and operation of human neurons. It's also referred to as neural networks or neural nets. The input layer of an artificial neural network, which is the first layer, receives input from external sources and forwards it to the hidden layer, which is the second layer. Each neuron in the hidden layer receives information from the preceding layer's neurons, computes the weighted total, and then sends it to the neurons in the next layer. These connections are weighted, which indicates that the impacts of the preceding layer's inputs are more or less optimized by assigning a different weight to each input. These weights are then modified during the training phase to improve the model's performance.

In artificial neural networks, artificial neurons, also known as units, can be found. These artificial neurons, which are stacked in a succession of layers, make up the entire Artificial Neural Network. Whether a layer includes a dozen units or millions of units, the complexity of neural networks is determined by the complexities of the underlying patterns in the dataset. An Artificial Neural Network typically contains an input layer, an output layer, and hidden layers.

The input layer gets information from the outside world that the neural network must analyze or learn.

An input layer and one or more hidden layers are connected one after the other in a fully connected artificial neural network. Each neuron receives information from neurons in the previous layer or the input layer. The output of one neuron becomes the input to other neurons in the network's next layer, and so on, until the last layer generates the network's output. The data is then turned into valuable data for the output layer after traveling through one or more hidden layers. Finally, the output layer generates output in the form of an artificial neural network's reaction to the input data.

In the majority of neural networks, units are linked to one another from one layer to the next. Weights are assigned to each of these relationships, which govern how much one unit influences another. As it travels from one unit to the next, the neural network learns more about the data, eventually providing an output from the output layer.

STATE-OF-THE-ART MODELS: GPT-3, GPT-4, AND BEYOND

OpenAI is back in the news, this time with the announcement that it is updating its viral ChatGPT with a new version named GPT-4. But when will it be ready, how does it work, and will it be usable?

ChatGPT is a machine learning (AI) tool that can answer questions, tell stories, compose essays, and even write code. The chatbot is so advanced that people are now seeing AI's true potential and how, for better or worse, it may define humanity's future. A free version of ChatGPT, developed by OpenAI in San Francisco, is accessible for anybody to use on the ChatGPT website. All you have to do to gain a login is sign up, and you'll be mining the depths of the AI model in seconds.

Since its release last year, ChatGPT's accessibility has attracted millions of users as well as considerable debate. Schools have already begun to prohibit ChatGPT because kids can use it to cheat, and some nations have barred their nationals from accessing the ChatGPT website. There are also numerous ethical and legal concerns when it comes to AI. In addition, the ChatGPT family is expanding. The free web version of ChatGPT is currently based on an enhanced model of GPT-3, but OpenAI has created an upgrade in GPT-4, which premium customers can access via ChatGPT Plus. Another version named 'ChatGPT Business' is also in the works, according to the business.

What Exactly are GPT-3, GPT-4, and ChatGPT?

OpenAI's GPT-3 (Generative Pretrained Transformer 3) and GPT-4 AI models for language processing are cutting-edge. They can generate human-like writing and have a wide range of applications, including language translation, language modeling, and text generation for chatbots. With 175 billion parameters, GPT-3 is one of the largest and most powerful language-processing AI models to date.

So far, the most prevalent use has been the creation of ChatGPT, a highly sophisticated chatbot. To demonstrate its most basic capability, we requested GPT-3's chatbot to write its own description, as seen above. It's a touch cocky, but it's absolutely truthful and, in my opinion, quite nicely written. In layman's terms, GPT-3 allows a user to provide a trained AI with a variety of written prompts. These can be queries, requests for a piece of writing on a topic of your choice, or a variety of other phrases.

It identified itself as a language-processing AI model before. This simply implies that it is a program that can understand human language as it is spoken and written, allowing it to comprehend the textual information it is fed and determine what to spit back out.

What is ChatGPT Capable Of?

With 175 billion characteristics, it's difficult to pinpoint what GPT-3 performs. As one may expect, the model is limited to language. It, unlike its brother Dall-E 2, cannot produce video, sound, or images but instead has a thorough knowledge of the spoken and written word.

This offers it a rather broad variety of abilities, from creating poems about sentient farts and cliché rom-com in parallel universes to explaining quantum theories in layman's terms and producing full-length research papers and articles.

While it can be entertaining to use OpenAI's years of study to get an AI to write horrible stand-up comedy scripts or answer questions about your favorite celebrities, its true power resides in its speed and comprehension of complex issues. ChatGPT can provide a well-written alternative in seconds, but we could spend hours researching, analyzing, and writing a paper on quantum mechanics.

It has limitations, and its software can become quickly confused if your prompt becomes too intricate or if you simply walk down a path that becomes a little too niche. It also cannot deal with thoughts that are too new. World events from the previous year will be faced with limited knowledge, and the model may occasionally offer inaccurate or confusing information.

OpenAI is also well aware of the internet's penchant for causing AI to produce dark, damaging, or biased content. ChatGPT, like its predecessor, the Dall-E image generator, will prevent you from asking inappropriate queries or requesting assistance with risky requests.

How Much Does ChatGPT Cost, And How Does It Work?

- Go to the ChatGPT website and sign up for an account.
- You must wait until your account is accepted (you can skip this step if you have a Dall-E 2 account).
- When you log in, you will be taken to a very simple page. You are given some sample prompts as well as information about how ChatGPT works.
- A text box is located at the bottom of the page. This is where you may ask ChatGPT any questions or provide prompts.
- Please keep in mind that the registering procedure requires you to supply a valid phone number. OpenAI states it requires a phone number to validate your account for security and that it is not used for any other purpose.
- Apple users can get the ChatGPT iOS software from the Apple software Store. There is currently no Android equivalent; however, OpenAI has promised that ChatGPT will be available on Android smartphones soon. In the meanwhile, Android users can still access the web version of ChatGPT through their search engines.
- ChatGPT is now available for free. However, OpenAI has already released ChatGPT Pro, a paid-for version with additional features.
- This version of the program will cost $20 (£16) per month and will provide customers with priority access, faster load speeds, and first access to upgrades and new features.

CHAPTER 3

DEEP DIVE INTO GPT-4

While GPT-4 is still hypothetical, we can predict various future developments and enhancements based on the GPT series' trajectory and trends in NLP research. To begin with, GPT-4 is expected to have a higher model size and capacity than its predecessors. Previous versions, such as GPT-3, demonstrated impressive capabilities with their huge model sizes. GPT-4 has the potential to outperform this scale by including an even higher number of factors. With this expanded capacity, the model would be able to capture and comprehend complicated language patterns at a higher level, resulting in more coherent and contextually relevant responses.

Another area where GPT-4 could improve is its capacity to comprehend fine-grained context. GPT-3 displayed an amazing knowledge of larger context within discussions, but GPT-4 could go even farther. GPT-4 could excel in capturing and utilizing more nuanced context by leveraging breakthroughs in attention mechanisms and contextual comprehension. This includes greater handling of ambiguous prompts, increased sensitivity to slight alterations in discourse, and the capacity to read complex requests appropriately.

GPT-4 may also continue to progress in terms of few-shot and zero-shot learning. Without significant training, these strategies allow models to generalize from a small number of samples or even generate outputs for whole new jobs. GPT-4 may have improved few-shot learning abilities, helping it to comprehend and adapt to new tasks with few examples. Zero-shot learning, in which the model generates replies for tasks that it has not been explicitly taught, could also be improved. GPT-4 would become more versatile and adaptable to a wider range of applications as a result of these advancements.

It should be noted that the specifics of GPT-4's capabilities and upgrades will only be known with certainty once it is officially published. The forecasts above are based on field trends and the GPT series' historical development. The actual features and developments of GPT-4, if they are realized, may differ from the aspirations indicated here.

ARCHITECTURE AND MODEL ENHANCEMENTS

Chat GPT4 Architecture

The development of the Generative Pre-trained Transformer (GPT) series has been one of the most significant developments in recent years as the world of artificial intelligence (AI) continues to evolve at a rapid rate. GPT-4, the most recent generation, has received a lot of attention for its capacity to generate human-like prose, which has a wide range of applications, from natural language processing to creative writing.

The Transformer model, first described by Vaswani et al. in 2017, is at the heart of GPT-4's architecture. The Transformer model transformed natural language processing by integrating self-attention mechanisms that enable the model to weigh the relevance of distinct words in a phrase based on their context. Because it can successfully capture long-term dependencies and interactions between words, this method allows GPT-4 to generate more coherent and contextually meaningful content.

The use of unsupervised pre-training is one of the fundamental advances in GPT-4's design. This method requires training the model on a vast corpus of unlabeled text data, such as books, articles, and websites. The algorithm learns to generate text by predicting the next word in a sentence based on the ones that came before it. This unsupervised pre-training enables GPT-4 to acquire a large amount of knowledge about language, syntax, and even actual facts, which it can subsequently use to fine-tune the model for specific tasks.

GPT-4's sheer size is another distinguishing feature. GPT-4 is substantially larger than its predecessor, GPT-3, and many other cutting-edge language models, with billions of parameters. This larger size enables GPT-4 to store and process more data, resulting in greater performance on a variety of applications. However, this raises concerns about computational resources and training time, as the model requires strong gear and prolonged training to reach its spectacular results.

The ability of GPT-4's architecture to execute few-shot learning is one of its most prominent features. This means that instead of thousands or millions of labeled data points, the model can learn to do new tasks with a small number of samples. This gives GPT-4 a substantial advantage over many other AI models in that it can be more easily adaptable to new jobs and domains, avoiding the need for time-consuming and costly data collection and labeling.

In addition to these advancements, GPT-4 benefits from a number of architectural changes made since the introduction of GPT-3. Advances in the self-attention mechanism, which helps the model to focus more effectively on relevant input, as well as optimizations in the model's training process, which help to prevent overfitting and increase generalization, are examples of these.

Despite its great powers, GPT-4 has certain limitations. One of the main issues about the model is that it has the ability to generate misleading or damaging information, as it can generate text that appears plausible but may not be true or acceptable. This has resulted in ongoing research into ways for managing and guiding the model's output, as well as efforts to build more strong evaluation measures for evaluating the quality and safety of the generated text.

What Are the Advantages and Improvements of GPT-4 Over GPT-3?

Language models are getting more sophisticated and powerful than ever before as artificial intelligence continues to advance at an unprecedented rate. The development of OpenAI's GPT series, with GPT-4 setting new benchmarks for natural language processing and interpretation, has been one of the most breakthrough advances in recent years.

Improved Language Comprehension and Generation

GPT-4's better understanding and creation of natural language is one of the most significant advances over GPT-3. This improvement in performance is mostly due to an increase in the number of parameters, which makes GPT-4 one of the largest and most powerful language models available. As a result, GPT-4 has a deeper awareness of context, semantics, and syntax, allowing it to produce more coherent and contextually appropriate responses.

Less Bias and Greater Fairness

AI algorithms frequently learn biases included in training data inadvertently, which might result in unforeseen repercussions when generating text or making judgments. With GPT-4, which features a more refined approach to bias mitigation, OpenAI has made great gains in tackling this issue. GPT-4, when compared to GPT-3, displays a significant reduction in both subtle and blatant biases by adding approaches such as rule-based rewards and counterfactual data augmentation, making it a more dependable and fair tool for a variety of applications.

Increased Integrity and Fewer Errors

The increased parameter count in GPT-4, together with enhanced training procedures, resulted in a model with higher fidelity and fewer errors. This suggests that GPT-4 is better at creating accurate and contextually relevant information, with a lower chance of delivering inaccurate or illogical responses. This enhancement considerably broadens GPT-4's possible uses, giving it a more reliable tool for activities requiring accuracy and precision, such as fact-checking, content development, and customer assistance.

Improved Capabilities for Few-Shot Learning

The ability of a model to grasp and perform new tasks with little exposure to examples is referred to as few-shot learning. GPT-3 was a pioneer in this area, while GPT-4 goes even further. The improved few-shot learning capabilities of GPT-4 enable it to accomplish tasks with even fewer examples, making it more adaptive and efficient in real-world applications. This advancement is critical for developers and enterprises who want to use AI but don't have access to massive amounts of labeled data.

Increased Multilingual Capability

GPT-3 was previously capable of processing many languages, but GPT-4 expands on this feature. GPT-4 can generate more accurate and contextually appropriate responses in a larger number of languages as its comprehension of many languages and their nuances grows. This advancement is crucial for organizations and developers who want to offer multilingual applications and services to a worldwide audience.

Expansion of Real-World Applications

GPT-4 advances have enabled new real-world applications that were either impossible or impractical with GPT-3. GPT-4's reduced bias and higher accuracy, for example, make it more suitable for sensitive jobs like medical diagnosis help, legal document analysis, and even combating disinformation. Furthermore, the expanded language production capabilities of GPT-4 have opened up new opportunities in creative domains such as content development, narrative, and poetry generation.

Improved Fine-Tuning Efficiency

One of the GPT models' primary characteristics is their capacity to be fine-tuned for specific purposes. The architecture enhancements in GPT-4 have made fine-tuning more accurate. The more efficient fine-tuning strength of GPT-4 enables developers to more easily and effectively adjust the model to specialized requirements. This capability enables GPT-4 to be quickly customized for a wide range of applications, from sentiment analysis to customer assistance, while reducing the resources and time required for optimization.

GPT-4 is superior to GPT-3

GPT-4 offers a substantial advancement in natural language processing and comprehension. GPT-4 outperforms its predecessor, GPT-3, in terms of language understanding, bias reduction, fidelity, few-shot learning, multilingual performance, real-world applications, and fine-tuning efficiency. These advancements have widened the breadth of AI applications, allowing developers and organizations to harness the power of advanced language models in new ways. As GPT-4 continues to reshape the AI landscape, we can anticipate even more revolutionary advancements and ideas that will shape how we interact with and benefit from artificial intelligence in the near future.

UNDERSTANDING GPT-4'S TRAINING METHODOLOGY

The GPT-4 language model from OpenAI has been making headlines in the artificial intelligence (AI) world. GPT-4 is a deep learning-based language model developed by OpenAI that can generate human-like writing from a prompt. Its architecture is built on the transformer network and was trained on a vast amount of text data.

GPT-4 is a machine learning model that generates text using natural language processing (NLP). It is trained on a vast corpus of text data and uses it to learn language structure. The model can then generate text that is comparable to the text on which it was trained.

GPT-4 learns language structure via a transformer network. This network is made up of several layers that process the input text. Each layer takes the preceding layer's output and utilizes it to generate a new output. This approach is continued until the model produces text that is similar to the text on which it was trained.

The transformer network can also be used to generate text in response to a prompt. The model will generate text that is comparable to the prompt when given one. GPT-4 is able to generate text that is more appropriate to the prompt than other language models.

GPT-4 is a remarkable model that can generate human-like text in response to a command. Its architecture is built on a transformer network, which enables it to learn the structure of language and generate text that is comparable to the text on which it was trained. As a result, GPT-4 is an extremely strong tool for natural language processing and text production.

How to Customise OpenAI's GPT-4 for Your Needs

1. Create a dataset of instances from which GPT-4 can learn. This dataset should contain examples of the type of writing that you want GPT-4 to produce.
2. Prepare the dataset. This comprises cleaning the text, tokenizing it, and formatting it in a GPT-4-compatible way.
3. Run GPT-4 on the dataset to train it. This can be accomplished by utilizing the OpenAI API or an open-source application such as Google Colab.
4. Customise GPT-4 for your specific task. This can be accomplished by modifying the model's hyperparameters or by employing transfer learning.
5. Put GPT-4 to the test on your unique task. This can be accomplished by comparing the output text to the original dataset or by employing a human evaluation.
6. Configure GPT-4 for your specific task. This can be accomplished by deploying the model to a cloud platform such as AWS or Google Cloud.

EXPLOITING GPT-4'S CAPABILITIES FOR VARIOUS APPLICATIONS

If GPT-4 were to be built with expanded capabilities, it might be used for a wide range of applications in several sectors. Here are a few examples of how possible GPT-4 developments could be used:

Understanding and Generating Natural Language

The improved fine-grained context comprehension and larger model size of GPT-4 may significantly improve natural language understanding and generation jobs. It could be utilized in chatbots and virtual assistants to deliver more accurate and contextually appropriate responses, resulting in more human-like interactions with AI systems. The extensive language-generating capabilities of GPT-4 may also find use in content creation, automatic summarization, and creative writing, where it may generate high-quality prose tailored to specific requirements or prompts.

Search and Personalised Recommendations

The greater contextual knowledge of GPT-4 could be used to provide more personalized suggestions and search results. It could deliver personalized suggestions for films, books, products, or other material by understanding the user's tastes and previous interactions. GPT-4's bigger model size could be used to interpret difficult questions and deliver more accurate and diversified search results, increasing the user's overall search experience.

Virtual Education and Learning

GPT-4, with its enhanced few-shot learning capabilities, has the potential to play a key role in virtual learning and education. It could accommodate various learning styles, provide personalized coaching, and provide explanations on a wide range of topics. GPT-4 might create interactive learning materials, respond to student inquiries, and provide feedback on assignments, creating an immersive and adaptive learning environment.

Assistance with Knowledge Discovery and Research

Because of its better language understanding and higher capability, GPT-4 could be a beneficial tool for knowledge discovery and research support. It could help academics analyze massive amounts of scientific literature, generate summaries, and provide insights into a variety of subjects. The ability of GPT-4 to interpret fine-grained context should help researchers navigate complex datasets and discover pertinent information more effectively.

Applications for Creativity

The enhanced language creation capabilities of GPT-4 could be used in creative fields such as storytelling, scriptwriting, and content generation for games and virtual worlds. It could help with character conversation, immersive storytelling, and dynamic content generation based on user interactions. The ability of GPT-4 to interpret and generate language at a more complex level may open up new avenues for AI-driven creativity.

It is crucial to note that many possible uses are speculative, based on GPT-4 advances. The actual value and use cases of GPT-4 would be determined by its specific features, capabilities, and the application domain needs in which it is deployed.

CHAPTER 4

HARNESSING THE POWER OF AI PLUGINS

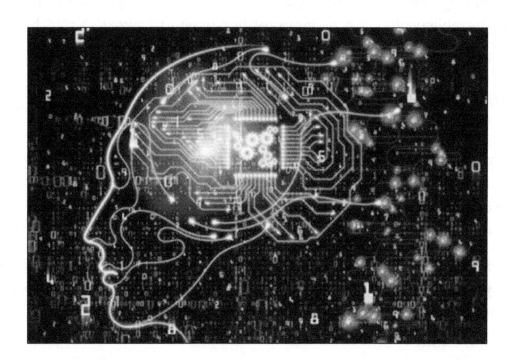

Harnessing the power of AI plugins can provide numerous benefits and offer up new opportunities in a variety of sectors. AI plugins are software components that incorporate artificial intelligence capabilities into current applications or systems, enhancing their usefulness and enabling sophisticated AI-driven features. These plugins are effective tools for increasing productivity, improving decision-making, automating chores, and providing vital insights.

Businesses can harness the capabilities of machine learning, natural language processing, computer vision, and other AI technologies by integrating AI plugins into applications rather than starting from scratch. An e-commerce platform, for example, may use an AI plugin to make personalized product recommendations, improving the user experience and driving sales. AI plugins in the healthcare business can aid in medical diagnostics, analyze patient data, and support healthcare workers in making informed treatment decisions. AI plugins can also help with content generation by automating summarization, translation, and sentiment analysis. AI plugins' flexibility and extensibility enable organizations to customize their apps to unique demands while leveraging cutting-edge AI capabilities without requiring large development resources.

However, while using AI plugins, it is critical to address potential ethical and privacy consequences. To secure sensitive information, data privacy and security must be properly maintained, and AI algorithms must be created and implemented responsibly to ensure fairness, transparency, and accountability. To maximize the benefits of these powerful technologies, it is critical to strike the correct balance between using AI plugin capabilities and preserving ethical issues. AI plugins may complement apps and systems with correct implementation and a human-centered approach, allowing organizations and individuals to do activities more effectively and make more informed decisions in today's AI-powered environment.

INTRODUCTION TO AI PLUGINS AND THEIR FUNCTIONALITY

AI plugins are software components that integrate artificial intelligence (AI) capabilities into current applications or platforms, therefore expanding functionality and improving user experiences. These plugins make use of the intelligence and automation provided by AI algorithms and models.

Here are some examples of common AI plugins and their functions:

Plugins for Natural Language Processing (NLP)

NLP plugins allow the software to understand and interpret human language. They can do text analysis, sentiment analysis, language translation, and chatbot functions. To analyze and comprehend textual data, NLP plugins employ techniques such as named entity recognition, part-of-speech tagging, and machine learning algorithms.

Plugins for Image and Video Recognition

These plugins analyze and interpret visual content using machine vision algorithms. Within photos or videos, they can recognize objects, faces, gestures, and scenes. Face recognition systems, object detection, content moderation, and augmented reality are just some of the applications for image and video recognition plugins.

Plugins for Speech Recognition and Synthesis

These plugins allow apps to understand and process spoken language. They transform spoken words into text and vice versa (speech recognition and speech synthesis). Speech recognition plugins are used in voice assistants, transcription services, and interactive voice response systems, whereas speech synthesis plugins are used in text-to-speech applications to generate human-like speech from text.

Plugins for the Recommendation System

These plugins use AI algorithms to deliver personalized suggestions to users, such as collaborative filtering or content-based filtering. To offer products, movies, music, or articles based on user interests and behavior, recommendation system plugins are often used in e-commerce platforms, streaming services, and content curation applications.

Plugins for Predictive Analytics

Machine learning algorithms are used by predictive analytics plugins to analyze historical data, detect patterns, and create predictions or projections. Predictive maintenance, demand forecasting, fraud detection, consumer behavior prediction, and risk assessment are all possible with these plugins.

Plugins for Sentiment Analysis

Sentiment analysis plugins examine text or social media data to assess the emotional tone or sentiment conveyed by users. They may categorize text as good, negative, or neutral, allowing applications to better comprehend public opinion, evaluate customer mood, and track brand reputation. To achieve accurate sentiment categorization, sentiment analysis plugins use machine learning models trained on labeled data.

Plugins for Chatbots

Chatbot plugins allow programs to connect with users in a conversational manner. They comprehend user inquiries and deliver relevant responses using natural language processing and machine learning techniques. To automate interactions and provide personalized advice, chatbots can be connected to a variety of platforms, including websites, messaging apps, and customer care systems.

These are only a few examples of AI plugins and their features. AI plugins allow developers to harness the power of AI without having to design complicated AI systems from the ground up.

They may be readily integrated into current apps, allowing developers to improve functionality and give consumers intelligent features.

POPULAR AI PLUGINS AND THEIR INTEGRATION WITH GPT-4

My knowledge as an AI language model is based on GPT-3.5, and I don't have particular information on GPT-4 or its integration with popular AI plugins because it exceeds my September 2021 knowledge threshold. However, I can provide you with an overview of some prominent AI plugins that have been widely utilized and integrated with AI models, such as GPT-3. It is crucial to note that the integration possibilities may change as fresh AI models and plugins become available. Here are a couple of such examples:

Transformers with Hugging Faces

Hugging Face Transformers is a popular natural language processing library that has been merged with GPT models. It offers a diverse set of pre-trained models for tasks such as text production, translation, sentiment analysis, and others. Integration with GPT-4 would most likely entail modifying the Transformers library to take advantage of the new model's expanded capabilities and features.

ChatGPT API by OpenAI

OpenAI provides APIs for developers to integrate GPT models, such as ChatGPT, into their applications. The API makes it easy to construct conversational agents, virtual assistants, and chatbot apps by providing a simple way to communicate with the model. Integration with GPT-4 would very certainly necessitate changing API endpoints and adjusting the integration process to match the new model.

AI on Google Cloud

Natural language processing, computer vision, and speech recognition are among the AI services provided by Google Cloud. These services can be combined with other AI models, including GPT, to improve application functionality. Integration with GPT-4 would almost certainly entail using the new model for tasks like text analysis, image recognition, and voice processing.

Cognitive Services on Microsoft Azure

Azure Cognitive Services offer a variety of artificial intelligence (AI) features that may be integrated into applications. Language understanding, audio recognition, and image analysis are all services that can be integrated with AI models like GPT to provide more advanced capabilities. The new model would most likely be used within the Azure Cognitive Services framework for integration with GPT-4.

AI Services from Amazon Web Services (AWS)

AWS provides artificial intelligence services such as natural language processing, image recognition, and audio analysis. These services can be combined with AI models such as GPT to enhance the intelligence of apps. Integration with GPT-4 would most likely include modifying AWS AI services to take advantage of the new model's capabilities.

It is important to note that the availability and integration possibilities for AI plugins can differ based on the model and platform used. It is encouraged to refer to the official documentation and resources supplied by the creators of the particular AI model or plugin for the most accurate and up-to-date information regarding the integration of AI plugins with GPT-4.

LEVERAGING AI PLUGINS FOR ENHANCED AI SYSTEM PERFORMANCE

AI plugins can be used to improve the performance of AI systems in a variety of ways. Here are some tips for using AI plugins to boost AI system performance:

Performing Computationally Intensive Activities Elsewhere

AI plugins can be used to outsource resource-intensive activities, such as complicated image or speech recognition, to specialized AI services or plugins. By delegating these activities to dedicated plugins or services, the main AI system can concentrate on its core functions while the plugins process the results.

Adding to Existing Models

AI plugins can supplement the existing AI system by adding new functionality or specialized capabilities. For example, if a natural language processing AI system lacks sentiment analysis capabilities, a sentiment analysis plugin can be incorporated to improve the system's comprehension of user sentiment. This enhancement boosts the AI system's overall performance and accuracy.

Increasing Data and Knowledge Sources

AI plugins can access other data sources, APIs, or databases to supplement the knowledge base of the AI system. The AI system can make better decisions and perform better by incorporating plugins that provide access to important data. A news aggregator AI system, for example, can incorporate plugins to fetch and analyze real-time news stories from numerous sources, ensuring it is always up to date with the most recent information.

Customization and Fine-Tuning

AI plugins can be used to fine-tune or customize the AI system's behavior to meet unique needs. Plugins may include changeable parameters or settings that allow users to tailor the AI system's behavior to their specific requirements. This adaptability allows the AI system to be more adaptive, accurate, and performant in a variety of situations.

Handling and Validating Errors

Plugins can help an AI system handle errors and validate input. An input validation plugin, for example, can validate the integrity and validity of user inputs before they are processed by the primary AI system, lowering the chance of incorrect or misleading outcomes. By implementing such plugins, the AI system can increase its reliability and performance by preventing errors at the beginning of the data processing process.

Updates and Continuous Improvement

AI plugins allow for ongoing upgrades and improvements to the AI system without requiring large changes to the core software. Updates to plugins may include bug fixes, performance improvements, or the incorporation of newer AI models. This method allows for incremental improvements and keeps the AI system current with the newest advances in AI technology.

AI plugins can help developers improve the performance, scalability, and diversity of AI systems. The specific plugins chosen, as well as the integration strategy, will be determined by the AI system's requirements, limits, and objectives.

CHAPTER 5

ETHICAL CONSIDERATIONS IN AI DEVELOPMENT

To address the possible impact on jobs and the workforce, ethical considerations in AI research are critical. As AI technologies improve, there is concern that job displacement and social disparities will result. Developers should prioritize methods to mitigate these negative consequences and ensure a smooth transition. This might entail investing in reskilling and upskilling programs for affected people, promoting job creation in AI-related industries, and encouraging collaboration between humans and AI systems to improve productivity and job satisfaction. Additionally, developers should maintain transparency and open communication with stakeholders in order to encourage awareness and address concerns about the influence of AI on the workforce.

Another important ethical problem is the possibility of AI systems being exploited maliciously or propagating harmful biases and discrimination. Developers must be cautious about creating and deploying AI systems that can be weaponized or utilized in ways that violate human rights and freedoms. This necessitates strong ethical rules and legal frameworks that govern AI use, ensuring that it is consistent with human rights, privacy, and social values. Regular audits and independent assessments can assist in identifying and mitigating any ethical concerns or unexpected repercussions that may arise as a result of AI system deployment. Collaboration among developers, politicians, ethicists, and other stakeholders is critical to addressing these ethical concerns and shaping AI development in a responsible and constructive manner.

ADDRESSING BIAS AND FAIRNESS IN AI SYSTEMS

Addressing prejudice and fairness in AI systems is a critical component of responsible and ethical AI research. Bias in AI systems can occur for a variety of reasons, including biased training data, algorithmic design choices, or the influence of social biases inherent in training data. Here are some significant issues and ways for addressing bias and promoting justice in artificial intelligence systems:

Training Data that is Diverse and Representative

It is critical to ensure that training data is diverse and representative of the population. Biased data can lead to biased AI models. Therefore, having extensive and inclusive datasets that appropriately represent all demographic groups and perspectives is critical.

Data Preparation and Cleaning

Before training AI models, it is critical to thoroughly pre-process and clean the data in order to discover and reduce biases. Anonymizing sensitive attributes, eliminating personally identifiable information, and carefully evaluating the data for potential biases are examples of procedures that can be used.

Fairness in Algorithms

AI algorithms should be built and tested to ensure fairness. Fairness measurements and tests can assist in identifying and quantifying biases in AI model output. Different concepts of fairness, such as demographic parity or equalized odds, can be used to drive the design and evaluation of algorithms to ensure equitable outcomes across different demographic groupings.

Auditing On a Regular Basis and Bias Assessment

Auditing AI systems for bias and conducting bias evaluations on a regular basis will assist in identifying and correcting any unfairness that may develop. This may entail assessing the impact of AI systems on various populations, monitoring for disparities, and making required improvements to remove biases.

AI Development Teams that are Diverse and Ethical

Promoting diversity and inclusiveness in AI development teams can provide a larger range of opinions and aid in bias reduction. Having diverse teams can aid in identifying and addressing biases that may be introduced accidentally during the development process.

Transparency and Comprehensibility

It is critical to promote transparency and explainability in AI systems. Users and stakeholders should have access to information about how AI systems make decisions, and any biases or limits should be disclosed. Explainable AI approaches can assist in providing insights into AI models' decision-making processes.

Monitoring And Feedback Loops Are Ongoing

Continuous monitoring and feedback loops are required to detect biases that may arise after implementation. User input and real-world performance data can aid in understanding and reducing any unexpected biases.

Frameworks for Regulation and Policy

Governments and organizations can play a critical role in building regulatory frameworks and regulations that require AI systems to be fair and accountable. These frameworks may contain data collecting and usage criteria, algorithmic fairness standards, and means for auditing and certifying AI systems.

To address prejudice and fairness in AI systems, a combination of technical, sociological, and legal approaches is required. By implementing these tactics, we can try to create more egalitarian AI systems and reduce biases that can perpetuate unfair outcomes.

PRIVACY AND SECURITY CONCERNS IN AI APPLICATIONS

When creating and implementing AI systems, privacy and security are important factors. Here are some critical considerations for ensuring AI privacy and security:

Data Security

AI systems frequently rely on vast volumes of data, and it is critical that this data be handled with the strongest privacy protection. To reduce the danger of data breaches or unauthorized access, use privacy-preserving techniques such as data anonymization, aggregation, and encryption.

Adhere to applicable data protection requirements, such as the European Union's General Data Protection Regulation (GDPR) or the California Consumer Privacy Act (CCPA) in the United States.

Consent with Knowledge

Get informed consent from people whose data will be used for AI training or evaluation. Allow individuals to make educated decisions about sharing their data by clearly communicating the purpose, extent, and potential risks of data usage.

Data Storage and Transmission Security

Ensure that data utilized in AI systems is stored and sent securely. To safeguard data from unauthorized access, alteration, or theft, use strong encryption techniques, secure storage systems, and strict access controls.

Privacy Safeguards for Users

AI applications should be designed with privacy in mind. Reduce the amount of personally identifiable information (PII) collected and only keep data that is required for the intended purpose. Use techniques such as differential privacy to add noise or disturb data to safeguard individuals' privacy while maintaining the AI system's functionality.

Use of Ethical Data

Establish explicit norms and policies for data ethics. Prevent data misuse, such as unauthorized profiling, discrimination, or invasion of privacy. Ascertain that AI systems are designed to benefit individuals and society as a whole while respecting individuals' privacy rights.

Deployment of a Secure Model

Take care to secure the infrastructure and systems involved while implementing AI models. To protect against potential attacks or exploits, use secure coding practices, regular software updates, and vulnerability checks.

Adversarial Assaults

Consider adversarial attacks that could be used to manipulate or fool AI systems. Evaluate the robustness of AI models in the face of hostile inputs and use strategies like adversarial training or input validation to improve their resistance.

Partnerships with third-party services

Consider the privacy and security practices of third-party services or partners in the AI ecosystem. Examine their security measures, data handling practices, and compliance with relevant privacy rules to verify that these relationships do not jeopardize the privacy and security of your AI system.

Auditing and Monitoring

Install monitoring systems to detect unauthorized access attempts, strange behavior, or data breaches. Audit AI systems on a regular basis for privacy and security compliance and repair any detected vulnerabilities or breaches as soon as possible.

Addressing privacy and security problems in AI applications necessitates a multifaceted and comprehensive strategy. Organizations may preserve user data, manage risks, and establish confidence among users and stakeholders by integrating privacy and security safeguards throughout the AI development lifecycle.

RESPONSIBLE AI USE AND GOVERNANCE GUIDELINES

A set of concepts and practices to ensure the ethical and responsible development, deployment, and use of artificial intelligence (AI) systems is called responsible AI use and governance guidelines. These guidelines are intended to address potential hazards and issues related to artificial intelligence technology while also promoting its beneficial and positive impact on society. Here are some of the most important components of responsible AI use and governance:

Fairness and Bias Reduction

Steps should be taken to ensure that AI systems are fair and unbiased. To avoid discrimination or unjust treatment based on criteria like as ethnicity, gender, or socioeconomic status, biases in training data, algorithms, and decision-making processes must be addressed.

Robustness and Security

AI systems should be built to be strong, dependable, and secure. This entails thorough testing, validation, and monitoring to detect and minimize risks and ensure that AI systems work as intended while causing no harm or unforeseen consequences.

Human Control and Oversight

Humans should retain ultimate control over AI systems, and AI should be developed to supplement rather than replace human decision-making. It is crucial to avoid scenarios in which AI systems make critical judgments without human input or comprehension.

Education and Public Awareness

It is critical to promote AI literacy and awareness among consumers, developers, and policymakers. It promotes a greater awareness of AI technology, its potential, and its societal impact, allowing for more informed decisions and responsible use.

Collaboration and Multi-Stakeholder Participation

Responsible AI guidelines should be developed and implemented with the collaboration and input of diverse stakeholders, including researchers, policymakers, industry professionals, and civil society organizations. This helps to guarantee that varied perspectives and expertise are taken into account.

It should be noted that responsible AI use and governance requirements may differ among countries, organizations, and circumstances. There are other frameworks and projects that provide more precise suggestions and principles for responsible AI use, such as the European Commission's Ethics Guidelines for Trustworthy AI and the Partnership on AI's Ethical and Social Impact of AI Principles.

CHAPTER 6

RESPONSIBLE AI DEVELOPMENT AND DEPLOYMENT

The ethical and socially conscious use of artificial intelligence is central to responsible AI development and deployment. It includes a variety of factors like justice, openness, accountability, and bias reduction. To ensure that AI systems treat humans fairly and avoid discriminatory consequences, developers and organizations must prioritize these elements. They should also prioritize human well-being, privacy and data protection, and the development of AI systems that improve human capabilities. Responsible AI development and deployment can help create trust, minimize harm, and maximize the positive impact of AI technology on individuals and society by following these principles.

The necessity for explainability and openness is a critical part of responsible AI development and implementation. AI systems should be built with clear explanations for their decisions and actions. This increases trust and enables consumers to understand the reasoning behind AI-driven decisions. Addressing biases in AI algorithms and decision-making processes is also critical. To ensure equitable treatment and the elimination of discriminatory practices, developers should carefully choose and pre-process training data, monitor for biases on a regular basis, and adopt mitigation methods. Responsible AI development and deployment can encourage the responsible and beneficial use of AI technologies by adhering to these principles.

BIAS MITIGATION AND FAIRNESS IN AI SYSTEMS

Bias reduction and fairness in AI systems are key components of guaranteeing the ethical and equitable usage of AI technology. AI systems have the ability to perpetuate or even amplify biases in the data on which they are taught, resulting in discriminatory outcomes and unfair treatment of individuals or groups. As a result, it is critical to solve these concerns in order to create AI systems that are unbiased, fair, and respectful of human rights. Some significant aspects and ways for bias prevention and fairness in AI systems are as follows:

Data Gathering and Pre-processing

Biases can arise as a result of biased or incomplete data. To provide representative and diverse datasets, the data collection process should be carefully considered. Before training the AI model, data pre-treatment techniques can be used to discover and reduce biases in the data.

Data Diversity in Training

Diverse training data helps to eliminate bias and improve the system's capacity to generalize to a larger population. Data from numerous demographic groups representing different genders, races, nationalities, ages, and socioeconomic origins must be included.

Bias Evaluation and Auditing

AI systems must be tested for bias on a regular basis. This entails examining the system's outputs for inequalities among demographic groupings. Auditing can assist in identifying biases, understanding their roots, and taking corrective actions.

Metrics And Evaluation of Fairness

Creating fairness metrics and evaluation procedures can aid in the measurement and quantification of biases in AI systems. These measures can help to improve algorithm design and training by providing insights into the fairness of the system's outcomes.

Techniques For Algorithmic Fairness

A variety of algorithmic strategies can be used to reduce prejudice and ensure fairness. These are some examples:

   a. Pre-processing techniques: Before training the model, modify the training data to remove or decrease biased patterns.
   b. In-processing techniques: During training, modify the learning algorithm to explicitly integrate fairness constraints or objectives.
   c. Post-processing techniques: After-training adjustments to the model's predictions to ensure fairness and reduce biases.

Transparent and Explainable

Transparency and explainability in AI systems can aid in the detection and correction of biases. By providing interpretable reasons for the system's judgments, it becomes easier to identify and correct biases.

Diverse and Inclusive

Building AI systems with justice in mind necessitates the formation of diverse and inclusive development teams. Involving people from varied backgrounds and viewpoints can help detect biases and make educated decisions to mitigate them successfully.

It is critical to recognize that obtaining complete justice in AI systems is a difficult and continual effort. Bias reduction and fairness efforts should be viewed as iterative and changing, necessitating continuous examination and refinement in order to address new difficulties and assure equitable outcomes.

TRANSPARENCY, EXPLAINABILITY, AND ACCOUNTABILITY IN AI

Transparency, explainability, and accountability are important characteristics to consider while developing and deploying AI systems. These principles attempt to ensure that AI systems are understandable and accountable for their decisions and acts and that individuals and society as a whole may trust them. Here is a more in-depth look at each of these principles:

Transparency

Making AI systems and their procedures visible and understandable to consumers, developers, and other stakeholders is referred to as transparency. It entails revealing how AI systems are constructed, what data they use, and how they make choices. Transparent AI systems allow users to understand why specific results occur, allowing them to develop trust in the technology.

1. Model transparency: Sharing information about the AI model's architecture, algorithms, and parameters can help users and experts understand how the system works.
2. Data transparency: By disclosing information about the training data, such as its sources, collection techniques, and potential biases, users can analyze the data quality and its impact on the system's outputs.
3. Process transparency: Defining the development and deployment process, including feature selection, training protocols, and evaluation criteria, can shed light on the system's dependability and limitations.

Explainability

Explainability focuses on delivering clear and interpretable explanations for AI system decisions. It assists users and stakeholders in comprehending the factors and rationale underlying the system's outcomes. Explainability is especially critical in high-stakes applications involving human lives, rights, or major resources.

1. Models with interpretability and transparency, such as rule-based systems or decision trees, can provide explicit explanations for each decision.
2. Local explanations: Explaining individual predictions or judgments made by the AI system might assist users in understanding how specific inputs influence the output.
3. Feature importance: Understanding the AI system's decision-making process can be aided by identifying and expressing the relevance of various features or aspects evaluated by the AI system.

Accountability

Accountability means holding AI systems and their engineers accountable for the consequences of their behavior. It entails developing procedures to rectify errors, biases, or negative outcomes induced by AI systems. Accountability frameworks aid in the proper management of the advantages and dangers associated with AI technologies.

1. Ethical guidelines and standards: Creating and adhering to ethical guidelines and standards can aid in the promotion of responsible AI practices and give a framework for accountability.

2. Regulatory oversight: Governments and regulatory organizations can adopt laws, regulations, and audits to guarantee that AI systems adhere to ethical and legal standards and are held accountable for their activities.

3. Redress mechanisms: Creating avenues for individuals to express concerns, seek redress, or question AI-driven judgments can aid in addressing potential biases, errors, or discriminatory consequences.

4. Human oversight: Keeping humans involved and in charge of crucial decision-making processes can offer an extra degree of responsibility and guarantee that AI technologies are used appropriately.

5. Ongoing review and improvement: Monitoring and analyzing AI systems on a regular basis, gathering user feedback, and implementing lessons gained into system upgrades are critical for preserving accountability and eliminating biases or errors.

Transparency, explainability, and accountability are critical components of responsible AI development, implementation, and use. Adhering to these principles contributes to the development of trust, the promotion of ethical AI practices, and the reduction of potential hazards and biases connected with AI technologies.

CHAPTER 7

FUTURE TRENDS AND EMERGING APPLICATIONS IN AI

Several major trends and developing applications in the field of AI can be expected in the future. One such trend is the growing integration of artificial intelligence (AI) with Internet of Things (IoT) devices. As more gadgets connect to the internet, AI algorithms will be used to analyze and interpret the massive amounts of data produced by these devices. This integration will allow for increased automation, predictive maintenance, and decision-making in a variety of domains, including smart homes, smart cities, and industrial settings.

The healthcare industry is another emerging application of AI. AI has the potential to transform healthcare by allowing for more accurate diagnoses, personalized treatment regimens, and more efficient healthcare management. Machine learning algorithms can analyze patient data, medical records, and genetic data to uncover patterns and provide insights for early disease identification and treatment. AI-powered robots and virtual assistants can also help with health care, monitoring, and rehabilitation. AI and healthcare have the ability to greatly enhance patient outcomes, streamline processes, and lower healthcare costs.

ADVANCES IN REINFORCEMENT LEARNING AND ROBOTICS

In recent years, developments in reinforcement learning and robotics have pushed the frontiers of what is feasible in autonomous systems. Here are some significant advances in these fields:

Learning with Deep Reinforcement

Deep reinforcement learning (DRL) tackles complicated issues by combining reinforcement learning with deep neural networks. Google DeepMind's AlphaGo, which defeated the world champion in the board game Go, and OpenAI's Dota 2 bot, which defeated professional gamers, are two examples of DRL's astounding triumphs. Robots may learn complicated behaviors and make judgments based on sensory information using DRL.

Sim-to-Real Conversion

The reality gap is a difficulty in reinforcement learning—the performance of a learned strategy in a simulated environment may not transition well to the real world. The advancement of sim-to-real transfer techniques aims to close this gap. Robots can more effectively transfer their learned policies to the physical environment by training in simulation and using domain adaptation methods, eliminating the requirement for substantial real-world training.

Reinforcement Learning with Multiple Agents

MRL (multi-agent reinforcement learning) is concerned with systems in which numerous agents interact and learn at the same time. MARL has applications in collaborative robotics, a field in which robots collaborate to achieve common goals. It has ramifications for self-driving cars, smart grid management, and multi-robot systems. MARL algorithm advancements allow agents to coordinate and learn from each other's experiences, resulting in more efficient and cooperative behavior.

Learning through Imitation

Robots learn through witnessing examples from human experts in imitation learning. Recent advancements in this field have concentrated on learning through a combination of expert demonstrations and trial-and-error reinforcement learning. This allows robots to learn complex abilities more quickly and with less investigation. Imitation learning is useful in fields such as robot manipulation, autonomous driving, and robotic surgery.

Perception of Robots

Perception is critical in robotics because it allows robots to perceive and interact with their surroundings. Computer vision and sensor technology advancements have resulted in considerable increases in perception skills. Deep learning approaches have been used to solve problems in perception, such as object recognition, semantic segmentation, and pose estimation. These developments allow robots to better comprehend their surroundings and make intelligent judgments based on visual input.

Learning with Positive Reinforcement

It is critical to ensure the safety of autonomous systems, especially in real-world applications. The goal of safe reinforcement learning approaches is to add safety limitations to the learning process, prohibiting robots from performing actions that could result in catastrophic outcomes. These methods include model-based uncertainty estimation, constraint optimization, and reward shaping. Robots can work safely in dynamic and uncertain contexts thanks to safe reinforcement learning.

Robotic Applications in the Real World

Reinforcement learning and robotics have found practical applications in a wide range of fields. In warehouse automation, for example, robots are trained to optimize order fulfillment operations. Robots in healthcare can be programmed to undertake tasks such as surgical procedures or patient care. Another popular application field is autonomous driving, in which reinforcement learning is used to train self-driving cars to manage difficult traffic scenarios. These real-world examples show how reinforcement learning and robots are having an increasing impact on efficiency, safety, and quality of life.

These are only a few instances of advancements in robotics and reinforcement learning. Continued research and development in these domains are projected to result in significant advances and accelerate the implementation of autonomous systems in a variety of industries.

AI IN HEALTHCARE, FINANCE, AND OTHER INDUSTRIES

AI has made substantial advances in a variety of fields, including healthcare, banking, and many more. Here's how AI is transforming certain industries:

Healthcare

Medical Imaging:

Artificial intelligence algorithms can analyze medical pictures such as X-rays, MRIs, and CT scans to help radiologists find and diagnose disorders. AI can increase the accuracy and efficiency of image interpretation and aid in the detection of early indicators of diseases such as cancer.

Drug Development:

By analyzing massive amounts of biological data, AI-powered systems aid in the identification and development of new medications. Machine learning algorithms can anticipate the efficacy and probable negative effects of novel medication candidates, thereby speeding up the drug discovery process.

Personalized Healthcare:

By analyzing specific patient data, such as genetic information, medical records, and lifestyle factors, AI enables personalized treatment programs. This enables healthcare providers to personalize therapies to each patient's specific needs and thereby enhance patient outcomes.

Virtual Assistants (VAs):

Chatbots and other AI-powered virtual assistants aid patients with common medical questions, provide basic healthcare information, and triage patients by assessing symptoms. They may provide service 24 hours a day, seven days a week, and respond quickly to non-emergency inquiries.

Finance

Detection of Fraud:

To detect fraudulent acts, AI algorithms can discover trends and anomalies in financial transactions. Machine learning models examine previous data to detect questionable transactions, thereby lowering financial losses and boosting security.

Trading Algorithms:

AI algorithms are capable of analyzing massive amounts of financial data, identifying trends, and making quick trading judgments. This enables automated trading systems to execute deals with little human interaction, maximizing investment strategies through speed and accuracy.

Risk Evaluation:

AI algorithms can evaluate loan applications, assess creditworthiness, and forecast financial market hazards. AI can give more accurate risk assessments for lending and investment decisions by analyzing varied data sources such as credit history, financial records, and market patterns.

Customer Support:

Chatbots and virtual assistants powered by AI improve customer service in finance. They can answer consumer questions, give personalized financial advice, and help with basic transactions, increasing customer happiness and decreasing wait times.

Manufacturing

Quality Assurance:

AI systems can monitor industrial processes in real time, analyze sensor data, and discover potential flaws or anomalies. This enables proactive quality monitoring and lowers the risk of defective products reaching customers.

Predictive Maintenance (PM):

Machine learning systems can analyze sensor data to determine when maintenance is required. Manufacturers may schedule maintenance tasks more efficiently, minimize downtime, and optimize maintenance costs by anticipating future equipment breakdowns.

Optimization of the Supply Chain:

AI supports supply chain process optimization by analyzing data on demand, inventory levels, transportation, and logistics. This assists manufacturers in streamlining operations, lowering costs, and improving overall efficiency.

These are only a few of the applications of AI in healthcare, banking, manufacturing, and other industries. AI technology's continuing growth promises to revolutionize procedures, improve decision-making, and open up new opportunities in a variety of industries.

BOOK 3

PROFITING ONLINE WITH GPT-4 & PLUGINS

CHAPTER 1

INTRODUCTION TO ONLINE MONEY MAKING

Earning money has traditionally been associated with and limited to the traditional 'offline approach. People are eager to earn money online to supplement their cash inflows as the Internet has taken over a significant portion of our lives.

Online earning is a means of producing money through the Internet. It involves owning a website, starting an online business, or pursuing other online earning opportunities available through the Internet. Earning money online is convenient because it does not require any investment or appropriate time management. Online earning is regarded as one of the best and most important methods of supplementing your primary income. We can define online earning as making money from various Internet sources.

OVERVIEW OF ONLINE BUSINESS OPPORTUNITIES

For many ambitious entrepreneurs, starting a business is a dream come true, but coming up with an idea and establishing your venture can be difficult. In the digital age, selling online – both products and services – can provide ambitious entrepreneurs with innovative, low-cost beginning possibilities. The trick is to match your hobbies, strengths, and skills to an internet company idea that can meet a market need while also growing into a profitable enterprise.

Whether you want to become a full-time entrepreneur or start a side business online, your product or service should meet a unique market demand. We are mentioning a list of online business opportunities.

Create a Blog and Earn Money from It

It is quite simple to start a blog, and there are numerous ways to monetize it. Displaying advertising using Google AdSense is one of the most common ways to monetize your blog.

While you may create a blog in about 30 minutes, it will require effort to make it a success. You will need to provide your audience with informative, amusing, and engaging content on a frequent basis.

Learn how to be an Affiliate Marketer

Affiliate marketers earn sales commissions by recommending the products or services of others. It is the best online company to start and earn money from.

The majority of affiliate marketers promote these items and services through their own blogs, websites, and email lists. To establish an audience, they must understand several internet marketing tactics, such as SEO, email marketing, social media marketing, and content marketing.

Make and Market Online Courses

If you are extremely skilled at something, why not educate others and make a living from it? Another common option to start an internet business is to sell online courses.

Many users choose to gain skills and knowledge rapidly by enrolling in online courses. With the help of LMS software, creating an online course has gotten much easier. These platforms enable you to create interactive courses with simple tools for managing classes, students, course material, and more.

Become an SEO Expert

SEO, or Search Engine Optimisation, assists website owners in increasing traffic from search engines. It is a talent that necessitates ongoing study and staying current with current trends. SEO specialists might establish their own businesses, work as freelancers, or work full-time for a firm.

Create a Recipe or Food Blog

Food and recipe blogs are a profitable blogging niche as well as an excellent online business possibility.

Food and recipe blogs earn cash through a variety of business methods, including Google AdSense, affiliate marketing, selling recipe books, and maintaining an online store.

You must be passionate about food and cooking. Because it is a competitive field, you must think of ways to make your food blog unique and engaging.

Learn to be a Graphic Designer

Graphic designers earn a living by developing graphics, business logos, website designs, sales pages, and other materials. This is a large sector with several business and employment prospects.

To become a graphic designer, you must first learn how to utilize professional design software such as AI Artist, Midjourney, Adobe Illustrator, Photoshop, and others. There are numerous vocational training institutes, colleges, and universities that provide courses to assist you in getting started.

Develop Your Skills as a Content Marketer

Content marketers assist businesses in marketing their products and services by creating relevant and interesting content. To attract clients, all businesses require content. The demand for content marketers is expanding and is not expected to decrease anytime soon.

Become a PPC Expert

PPC stands for Pay-Per-Click advertising, in which advertisers pay for their advertisements only when users click on them. However, not all business owners understand how to conduct these initiatives efficiently and profitably.

KEY CONSIDERATIONS FOR PROFITABLE ONLINE VENTURES

Whether you wish to create a new internet business or reinvent an existing one, it is critical to understand that business success does not depend on having a revolutionary idea or selecting a market niche with minimal competition but on adhering to particular criteria.

In fact, inventing novel products or services that have never been tested before, or selecting a market sector with fewer competitors, is the worst idea imaginable. Because you have no proof that certain items, services, or markets exist. As a result, the best thing you can do to build a successful firm is to focus on specific success criteria, such as:

Choosing a Niche

Finding a specific niche and a way to attract clients are two key parts of any internet business. For example, if you choose a traditional company area, such as retailing, you can attract clients by establishing retail-specific and user-friendly web design elements and employing cutting-edge technology. This is how you will set your company out from the competitors.

Choosing the Best Business Concept

Choosing a topic that everyone understands allows you to expand your business in a matter of months. On the other hand, if you go for a new, revolutionary notion, you'll have to invest in educating an entire market. Simply, this may make or kill your company.

Offering High-Quality Goods and Services

If you want to get into and continue in business, you must provide high-quality products and services to your clients. To build a successful firm, you must first identify and adjust to minor details.

Having a Good Customer Relationship

Building good relationships with your clients is a simple recipe for growing and sustaining your business. Customers who are devoted to you can help you market and sell your products and services faster and easier than you think.

Increasing the Visibility of Your Brand

Because you are preparing to launch an internet business, one of the things you should consider is brand visibility. Making your brand visible essentially implies promoting your company over the Internet.

MONETIZATION MODELS AND STRATEGIES

A monetization strategy is a strategy for generating revenue through your platform, audience, content, or other means. There are numerous monetization strategies. Selling platform access, ad space, in-app purchases, and other methods are among the most frequent.

Great monetization methods are always evolving in response to the company's goals, which are also changing. They should also be adaptable enough to change in response to time, market, and users.

Apps for a Fee

Users used to have to pay for mobile apps when mobile app shops were first introduced. This was the leading app monetization approach employed by businesses at the time. That's difficult to believe, isn't it? In-app purchases and advertisements arrived later.

Today, there are various types of digital products where the paid app model is still quite effective:

Apps for productivity, photo and video editing, navigation, and utility.

Purchases Made In-App

One of the simplest methods for an application to generate revenue is to charge users for additional features or purchases that they may make once they begin using it.

In-app purchases can provide your users with additional premium features while keeping the primary product free (this is similar to the freemium model). This allows you to establish deeper interaction with your audience and inspire clients to purchase more functions once they understand the value they receive from your digital product.

Advertising within the App

Offering ad placements within your digital product is another prevalent method of revenue. Today, mobile app advertising is a major trend, and many applications employ it.

Affiliate Promotion

Affiliate marketing is an intriguing method of monetizing a mobile app. In the context of mobile apps, affiliate marketing means that you are paid a commission fee each time a user downloads the app or does a specified action via a link within your app.

Fee for Subscription

Many forms of digital products, including mobile applications, games, and Software as a Service (SaaS), use the subscription model.

Product Licensing

On the one hand, subscription-based streaming services such as Netflix and Spotify acquire licensed material (such as film or music) from third parties. Shazam, on the other hand, is frequently licensed to other companies in order to boost its revenue stream. You can, of course, license your patented technology to others. Data as a product or API as a product, for example, are both viable approaches to monetizing digital goods that use data, features, and APIs.

Corporate Sponsorships

You enter into an advertising connection with a single advertiser when you use the sponsorship model. A sponsor can appear as an icon or cover a greater piece of the UI of your app. You can also use the app splash screen for this, which is shown to abusers immediately after the application launches. Push alerts are also an option.

Crowdfunding

Crowdfunding services such as Indiegogo, Kickstarter, and GoFundMe are popular ways to monetize digital items.

However, before you go in, keep in mind that the revenue gained is uncertain. You also have no assurances about the consistency of your revenue stream. This channel is an excellent source of additional revenue. It is not a good idea to rely on it as a primary source of income.

CHAPTER 2

LEVERAGING GPT-4 FOR PROFITABLE ONLINE VENTURES

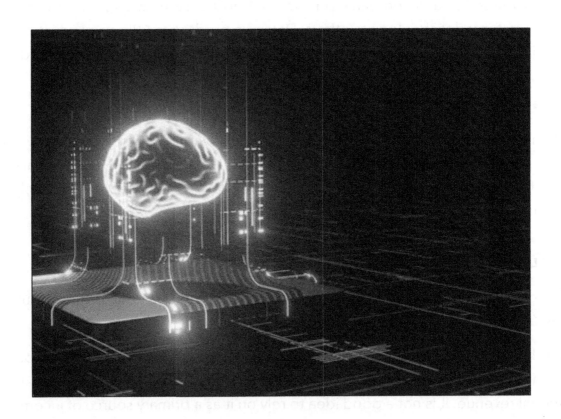

G PT-4 has emerged as a sophisticated language model with enormous potential as AI continues to improve. It combines natural language processing and creation to generate human-like text, making it an invaluable tool for a wide range of companies and individuals. Individuals can take advantage of creative revenue prospects in the AI era by exploiting GPT-4's capabilities.

GPT-4 is at the forefront of language modeling, with complex algorithms and vast datasets that allow it to interpret and generate high-quality text. It has a strong contextual awareness, making it an excellent tool for a variety of applications. Now, let's look at ten methods to use GPT-4 to make money:

USING GPT-4 FOR CONTENT CREATION AND MARKETING

Staying ahead of the curve in the ever-changing world of digital marketing is critical for firms to keep their competitive advantage. GPT-4, the most recent iteration of OpenAI's generative pre-trained transformer, has changed the way marketers approach content production, strategy, and optimization. This cutting-edge artificial intelligence (AI) model has unrivaled capabilities, making it an important asset in the field of digital marketing.

Articles and Blog Posts

GPT-4 digital marketing has brought up new avenues for writing blog posts and articles that attract readers' interest. The powerful natural language processing capabilities of GPT-4 enable it to generate well-researched, instructive, and interesting material. GPT-4 may generate a whole article matched to your audience's preferences by inputting a few human language keywords or a topic. This not only saves time but also guarantees that the content is up-to-date and relevant.

Landing Pages and Ad Copy

An effective digital marketing strategy requires engaging ad language and compelling landing sites. Marketers may use GPT-4 to generate ad copy that resonates with their target demographic, optimizing ad performance and conversion rates. Similarly, GPT-4 can assist in the creation of landing pages that successfully explain the value proposition and motivate people to take the desired action, such as subscribing to a newsletter or making a purchase.

Email Marketing

Email marketing is still an important tool for organizations to use in order to retain relationships with clients and nurture leads. The capacity of GPT-4 to generate tailored, engaging email content has the potential to greatly enhance open rates, click-through rates, and conversions. GPT-4's model can modify email content to match individual preferences and pain areas by evaluating user data, making each email feel more personal and relevant to the recipient.

Analysis And Research of Keywords

GPT-4 digital marketing is changing the way marketers handle keyword research and analysis. The powerful algorithms in GPT-4 can identify relevant keywords and evaluate their search volume, competition, and ability to drive organic traffic. GPT-4 assists organizations and enterprises with search engine optimization by developing content that ranks better on search engine results pages, ultimately increasing visibility and gaining more potential customers.

Optimization of Web Pages

On-page optimization is essential for increasing search engine ranks and improving user experience. By examining the structure, readability, and keyword usage, GPT-4 can help marketers optimize their content. This involves making suggestions for enhancements like writing catchy titles and meta descriptions, improving header tags, and strategically putting keywords throughout the content. GPT-4 can also assist with image optimization, making sure that images have meaningful alt tags and are correctly compressed for faster page load times.

Curation of Content

It takes time to curate high-quality, engaging social media posts and material for social media sites. GPT-4 technology makes this process easier by suggesting suitable content based on your target audience's interests and preferences. This guarantees that your social media channels and social media marketing are continually stocked with information that is relevant to your followers and potential consumers, hence increasing engagement and brand exposure.

Participation of the Audience

Engaging your audience on social media channels is critical for creating strong relationships and brand loyalty. GPT-4 can assist you with managing and optimizing audience engagement by evaluating user interactions, recommending answers to comments and messages, and spotting engagement trends. This enables organizations and enterprises to keep an active social media presence while responding to client issues and establishing a community around their brand.

Hashtag Investigation

Hashtags are essential for enhancing the visibility and reach of your social media content. By evaluating trends, user preferences, and industry-specific keywords, GPT-4 digital marketing enables marketers to determine the most effective hashtags for their content. You can ensure that your content reaches a bigger audience by integrating these hashtags into your social media postings, improving interaction and generating growth for your brand.

AI-POWERED CUSTOMER SERVICE AND SUPPORT SYSTEMS

Customer service is an important factor for 96% of consumers worldwide when determining whether or not to stay loyal to a company.

The key to offering real-time service for customer support platforms is artificial intelligence. Furthermore, this technology has the ability to change how customer service solutions are created.

Use Artificial Intelligence to Classify Support Tickets

You may simply categorize customer support tickets using automatic tagging techniques. This means that you add labels to your data to help structure it and make it easier to process. You can categorize your tickets using numerous tags.

You could, for example, tag your tickets based on the feature to which they pertain. Each ticket is reviewed and classified as referring to a certain feature, and your team now has a better understanding of what is causing problems for your users.

Use artificial intelligence to perform sentiment analysis on consumer surveys and comments.

You can assess consumer sentiment if your customer surveys include open-ended responses. The simplest categorization you can do here is to determine if a response is:

Positive Negative

You can use Sentiment Analysis to determine which aspects of the client experience have the greatest emotional impact.

Use Artificial Intelligence to Evaluate Text

You can evaluate text, such as customer support queries and competitor reviews, in the same way that you may analyze ticket sentiment. Simply enter the tags you wish the AI model to use while analyzing and categorizing your text, as shown below.

Make Use of an AI Customer Service Chatbot

Many firms now use chatbots to answer basic questions based on data from internal systems. This covers delivery dates, owed sums, order status, and other information.

Your consumers will be able to get answers to their questions more quickly and simply if you create an AI-powered chatbot to answer frequently requested inquiries with customer-specific information. As a result, customer support personnel may focus on more complicated issues and give a better overall experience while saving operating costs.

Use Artificial Intelligence to Provide Multilingual Help

You can detect languages and respond in your user's preferred language using automated technologies. When you have a global product, multilingual customer service can help you attract and retain customers. You can convert them into ardent brand fans by supporting them in reaping greater benefits from your products or services in a language that they understand.

PERSONALIZATION AND RECOMMENDATION ENGINES WITH GPT-4

The rise of artificial intelligence (AI) has transformed several industries, including recommender systems. The introduction of ChatGPT-4, a cutting-edge AI language model, is destined to alter the future of recommender systems, providing unrivaled personalization and customer delight. This article examines ChatGPT-4's impact on the future of recommender systems and how it will improve AI-driven personalization and user pleasure.

Recommender systems have become an essential part of our daily lives, assisting us in navigating the vast amount of information available online. These systems, which range from e-commerce platforms to streaming services, construct individualized recommendations based on our tastes, browsing history, and other data factors. Traditional recommender systems, on the other hand, frequently fall short of providing highly tailored experiences since they rely on relatively simple algorithms and limited data.

ChatGPT-4: A New Era of Recommender Systems

Enter ChatGPT-4, a cutting-edge AI language model with the potential to transform recommender systems. ChatGPT-4 can read and generate human-like writing by combining natural language processing (NLP) and deep learning techniques, making it a perfect tool for improving the personalization and effectiveness of recommender systems.

The Advantage of ChatGPT-4

The capacity of ChatGPT-4 to understand and handle complicated user inquiries is one of the primary advantages of putting it into recommender systems. Unlike typical systems that rely on keyword matching or collaborative filtering, ChatGPT-4 can understand human language nuances, allowing it to offer more accurate and relevant recommendations. For example, if a user requests a movie recommendation based on a specific subject or mood, ChatGPT-4 can assess the request and present a list of relevant possibilities based on the user's interests and viewing history.

The Dynamic Learning of ChatGPT-4

Furthermore, ChatGPT-4's deep learning capabilities allow it to learn and adapt to users' preferences over time. ChatGPT-4 may assess user behavior and comments as they interact with the recommender system to refine its recommendations, ensuring that they remain relevant and interesting. This dynamic learning approach improves not only personalization but also long-term user pleasure and loyalty.

The Conversational Approach of ChatGPT-4

ChatGPT-4's capacity to generate authentic, conversational responses is another key feature. Traditional recommender systems sometimes deliver recommendations in a list format, which consumers may find impersonal and overwhelming. ChatGPT-4, on the other hand, may communicate with users in a more interactive and human-like manner, making the suggestion process more pleasurable and engaging. This conversational approach can also assist users in discovering new material or goods that they may not have considered otherwise, thus enhancing user satisfaction and increasing the possibility of conversions.

The Power of ChatGPT-4's NLP Capabilities

Furthermore, the extensive NLP capabilities of ChatGPT-4 can be used to evaluate user-generated information, such as reviews and ratings, in order to extract significant insights and improve the overall quality of suggestions. ChatGPT-4 can recognize patterns and trends in user feedback by analyzing the sentiment and context behind it. These patterns and trends may then be utilized to fine-tune the recommender system, ensuring that it remains up-to-date and relevant to users' needs.

CHAPTER 3

EXPLORING AI PLUGIN OPPORTUNITIES

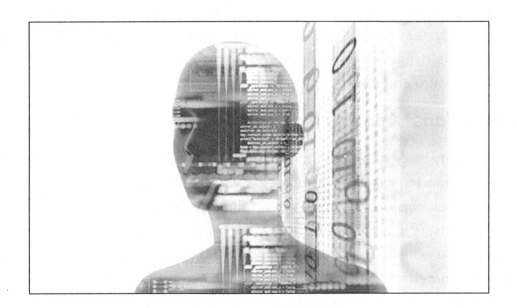

ChatGPT develops as a potent tool for creating human-like responses in conversational AI applications as the science of natural language processing advances. Developers have created the concept of plugins to further extend their capabilities and enhance their functionality. We'll look at what ChatGPT plugins are, how they operate, and why they're useful in this chapter. We will also provide step-by-step guidance for installing plugins, which will open up a world of limitless possibilities for your ChatGPT instance.

IDENTIFYING PROFITABLE AI PLUGIN NICHES

Artificial intelligence (AI) has quickly developed to become a dominant force in a variety of industries, influencing how businesses and individuals work. The market for AI plugins, applications, or extensions meant to add AI capabilities to existing platforms or systems has witnessed tremendous growth. They are capable of a wide range of functions, including process automation, trend prediction, and experience personalization. Identifying successful AI plugin categories is thus a rewarding opportunity for both corporations and developers.

Evaluating the Profitability of AI Plugin Niche

Profitability in AI plugin niches is defined mostly by the need for specific solutions, the competition of the niche, and the product's ability to grow. As a result, market research is the first and most important step in this endeavor. Businesses must investigate emerging trends, technological breakthroughs, and changes in consumer preferences. They should also think about market size, growth prospects, and entry hurdles.

Identifying Gaps and Opportunities in Customer Needs

Understanding client demands is essential for locating profitable niches. A profitable AI plugin is one that solves a genuine problem or improves a user's experience. Businesses can see these chances by communicating with potential customers, reading reviews and feedback on comparable products, and staying current on industry news and trends.

Profitable Niche

Content creation is one of the most potential markets for AI plugins. Because of the growing demand for information across several platforms, this area has received a lot of attention. AI plugins, which provide features such as AI authoring, graphic design, and video editing, can aid in the automation of the content creation process. These plugins save businesses and content creators time and effort, making them an appealing investment.

Artificial Intelligence for E-commerce Optimization

Another area where AI plugins can be quite valuable is e-commerce. They can aid in the improvement of product suggestions, the prediction of consumer behavior, the management of inventories, and the optimization of pricing methods. As more firms transition to e-commerce, the demand for such plugins is expected to rise.

Artificial Intelligence for Personalized Learning Experiences

AI has transformed education by providing personalized learning experiences. Artificial intelligence (AI) plugins that customize learning materials to the learner's pace, knowledge level, and interests are becoming increasingly popular. This type of plugin is compatible with learning management systems and e-learning platforms.

Artificial Intelligence for Healthcare Solutions

AI plugins are transforming healthcare, making this an especially profitable sector. These plugins can help with a variety of activities, including medical picture analysis, disease progression prediction, and administrative work automation. Given the sensitivity of healthcare data, these plugins must also prioritize security and privacy, imposing a high cost of entry that may hinder competition.

AI for Financial Predictive Analysis

AI plugins for predictive analysis are becoming increasingly popular in the financial sector. These technologies can assist in forecasting market trends, risk management, and trading automation. Despite the fact that this is a competitive sector, the strong demand for these solutions makes it a valuable subject to investigate.

DEVELOPING AND MARKETING AI PLUGINS

The proliferation of Artificial Intelligence (AI) across numerous industries has created opportunities for the development and marketing of AI plugins. These plugins improve existing applications and platforms by incorporating AI capabilities. Identifying a need, development, testing, launching, and promotion are all steps in the process of building and selling AI plugins.

The first step in creating an AI plugin is identifying a market need that your product can fill. Conducting market research to understand industry trends, client pain points, and competition products is part of this process. It is critical to create a unique selling proposition (USP) that distinguishes your plugin from the competition.

AI Plugin Creation

The next phase is development after identifying a need. This includes developing and coding the plugin architecture. It is critical to adhere to best practices for AI development, such as employing the appropriate AI models, protecting data privacy, and considering scalability and integration with other systems. Choosing the correct AI technologies and frameworks, such as TensorFlow or PyTorch, for machine learning capabilities is also part of the development process.

Putting the AI Plugin to the Test

Thorough testing is essential to ensuring that your AI plugin performs as planned and is bug-free. It should go through a series of tests, including functionality, integration, and performance testing. It's also a good idea to conduct user testing to receive feedback on the plugin's usability and efficacy.

Activating the AI Plugin

The next stage is to launch the plugin after it has been written and tested. This includes creating product documentation, establishing a customer support system, and determining price models. It's critical to select the correct distribution channels for your AI plugin, which could include a plugin marketplace, your company's website, or software distribution platforms.

Promotion and Marketing

Marketing and promotion are the final steps in the process. Content marketing, social media marketing, email marketing, search engine optimization (SEO), and partnerships with influencers or other businesses are all effective marketing tactics. In your marketing materials, you must emphasize the benefits and unique characteristics of your AI plugin. Demos, tutorials, and case studies can also help to demonstrate the value of your plugin.

Continuous Enhancement

The process does not end with the launch. The AI plugin may be continuously improved by gathering and evaluating user feedback on a regular basis. To guarantee that your plugin remains relevant and competitive, you must keep up with technical changes and changing customer needs.

COLLABORATIONS AND PARTNERSHIPS IN THE AI PLUGIN ECOSYSTEM

Welcome to the advent of an era in which artificial intelligence (AI) is the new frontier of software development, and collaborations are critical to progress. ChatGPT plugins, similar to an iPhone's App Store, are pushing a paradigm shift in the AI environment.

The Advent of ChatGPT Plugins

The recent alpha release of ChatGPT plugins by OpenAI heralds a new age of open AI development. These plugins allow for easy integration with third-party programs and make it easier to create APIs to extend ChatGPT's functionality. The barrier to entry into the AI area has been greatly reduced as a result of this advancement, encouraging a community of diverse and imaginative developers.

Democratizing AI Development through ChatGPT Plugins

ChatGPT plugins have the ability to change the way software is created. Certain plugins, for example, could automate the production of test cases or the analysis of algorithms, speeding workflows and enhancing productivity. Furthermore, plugins can considerably improve the interface between people and AI, reducing interactions and increasing the efficiency of procedures.

The Transformative Impact of ChatGPT Plugins on Software Development

The field of developer collaboration plugins is a notable area of expansion. Multiple developers and AI equivalents are brought together in the same environment by these tools. This setup is analogous to providing developers with a 3D printer, providing them with the necessary building elements to innovate and create.

Fostering Real-time Developer Collaboration with ChatGPT Plugins

These collaborative plugins, in essence, allow developers to collaborate with AI models, allowing them to tweak and optimize AI-generated code to match their specific needs. Developers can therefore concentrate on high-level design and decision-making, resulting in more inventive and stable software solutions.

The Evolution of Developer Collaboration with AI

Incorporating ChatGPT plugins into the software development process helps stimulate developer inventiveness. It allows students to experiment with various AI-generated components and design patterns, fostering innovation and thinking beyond the box.

CHAPTER 4

MONETIZING AI APPLICATIONS AND SERVICES

The generating of revenue from an AI initiative, product, or service is referred to as AI monetization. Unlike traditional hardware and software goods, which may be sold for a one-time cost with multi-tiered service and support contracts, AI requires a more complex model that acknowledges its worth over time and scales with its usage. In other words, selling what your technology provides for your consumers across a continuous time horizon is more important than selling your technology itself.

BUILDING AND SELLING AI-POWERED PRODUCTS

AI has numerous applications in a range of industries. The initial stage for any AI startup should be to determine its product line and market positioning. What issues are you attempting to resolve? What will your products accomplish? How can your AI technology differentiate itself from similar items on the market?

Once you've determined what your products will do and what purpose they will fulfill, it's time to determine your market positioning. Understanding your market positioning aids in the development of a successful marketing plan, which is critical for a bootstrapped firm.

The following steps are involved in determining your market positioning:

Determine the elements that distinguish your AI goods from the competition. These distinctions must represent values or characteristics that customers require or desire. Furthermore, they should be unique to your company; clients should only be able to obtain them while working with your AI technology.

Concentrate on the market segment (and clients) that you best service. Your product should not be a one-size-fits-all answer; instead, it should speak to a specific audience and sell them solutions that are relevant to the problems they are facing.

Define Your Ideal Client

Every brand has a target market. This is the person in mind when developing your AI product. Before marketing AI technology, AI businesses must first determine who their ideal clients are. Your ideal consumer is not simply encapsulated in a broad statement such as "we sell AI software to the farming industry." You must be as detailed as possible. "Our Company, for example, develops AI analytics software for wheat farmers that collects temperature, growth, yield, and other data."

Concentrate On the Customer and Their Issue

The majority of AI firms fail because they are overly focused on the technology underlying their ideas. Your ideal consumer doesn't care how you built your technology as long as they know it can solve their problems - and here is where the real money is.

When selling your AI solution by highlighting the technology behind it, the best you can expect from a potential lead is casual attention. However, in order to convert these leads, you must explain how your AI technology solves their concerns.

Customer Issues can be Identified By:

Understanding the environment, the customer's operations, the organizational structure, the business goals, and the broader industry difficulties.

Discover a customer's true difficulties (rather than the ones you believe they have) or assist them in discovering their own problems. Measure the issue to ensure that your consumers understand exactly how your AI solution solves their issue.

Create a Sales Strategy

You understand your product line, market positioning, ideal customer, and the problem your consumers are experiencing. The last stage is to create a sales plan that effectively communicates your value proposition. A sales strategy is also essential for launching your growth strategy and remaining competitive.

A sales plan for AI companies provides direction and defined goals for the company. A solid sales strategy will incorporate key performance indicators (KPIs), sales procedures, team structure, product positioning, sales tactics, buyer personas, and growth objectives.

You can accomplish this by:

Using AI to demonstrate the ROI for businesses. Most firms recognize AI as a game-changing technology, but few can justify the investment to key decision-makers. Educate your prospects on how to fully utilize AI solutions, including measures for measuring the impact of AI in their organizations.

Effectively communicate your startup's AI to stakeholders so that by the end of your presentation, they comprehend the benefits. Make sure your pitch is non-technical so that your message does not get buried in technical jargon.

AI Products that Add Value

Finally, any firm looking to sell AI technology must provide value to clients. Once you've established a clear narrative and a case for your AI, sell your clients value by setting expectations about the value you'll provide.

From the start, your consumers should understand exactly what your AI technology is capable of. This not only helps you develop a trustworthy brand, but it also enables for more widespread adoption of your AI technology.

PROVIDING AI CONSULTING AND TRAINING SERVICES

Artificial intelligence consultancy is the process through which AI developers and specialists assist businesses from many industries in adopting AI technologies to achieve their objectives. This is easier said than done because it entails a number of actions and is a lengthy process.

AI consulting firms have a variety of tasks and duties, including assisting organizations in making the most use of their resources.

Finding ways to cut costs without sacrificing quality:

- AI application design, integration, customization, and upkeep
- Training staff to use tools efficiently for day-to-day work, developing future strategies for the business's growth and expansion, and so on.

Let's take a closer look at the numerous services provided by AI consulting firms to grasp the significance of their presence in your corporation. Many consulting firms provide offshore services to organizations all over the world.

Strategy Development

The first stage is to develop an AI strategy or plan of action for an organization. Here, the AI consultants will meet with clients in-depth to identify areas best suited for AI integration. These are then ranked to create a list of the tools needed for the adoption process.

The emphasis is on determining the best path to take in order to build the necessary IT infrastructure and data pipelines to integrate AI technologies with existing legacy systems. When developing a strategy, factors such as resource availability, investment cost, project duration, and so on are taken into account.

Assessing Processes and Potential Outcomes

Many AI initiatives fail or are incomplete owing to a lack of review. Whether a company wants to construct an AI application from scratch or customize an existing one, AI experts will first assess the process's viability and potential outcomes. These AI professionals will assist firms in selecting commercially viable and successful projects. This lowers the chance of failure and investment loss.

Deployment and Implementation

The AI consulting firm now bears the primary responsibility for implementing and deploying the project (developing, integrating, modifying, etc.) in accordance with the authorized plan.

For example, if a company wishes to use chatbots to aid customer service representatives, the AI consulting team will develop the framework required to set up AI chatbots and automate their responsibilities at the helpdesk.

Training and upkeep

Some AI consulting firms also provide training. After all, the end user/employee must understand how to utilize the application. Training sessions are held to teach personnel about the new AI application's features and how to cope with problems.

In addition, if the organization desires, the consulting firm can continue to provide maintenance services. This means that AI professionals continuously verify the systems for flaws and enhance the features to ensure that they provide the most recent and anticipated services.

Compliance and Governance

The AI consulting firm is also in charge of ensuring that the artificial intelligence systems developed/customized for the enterprise are compliant and adhere to worldwide requirements. As part of the process, ensure data security and implement data governance mechanisms or standards. In organizations that operate with extremely secret data, AI consultants may need to implement numerous protection levels.

CREATING SUBSCRIPTION-BASED AI PLATFORMS AND MARKETPLACES

In a world where Netflix, Spotify, and Amazon Prime reign supreme, the concept of subscription models is as familiar as your favorite song on repeat. Subscription-based AI platforms take a leaf from the same book, providing a plethora of AI services in return for a recurring fee.

Imagine having an array of AI solutions at your fingertips, ready to tackle anything from data analysis to content generation, all for a monthly or annual subscription. Much like subscribing to a streaming service for unlimited movies and shows, businesses and individuals can now subscribe to AI platforms for limitless access to AI solutions. It's like having a Swiss Army knife of AI tools in your pocket!

Advantages of Subscription-based AI Platforms

Subscription-based AI platforms are like a magical wardrobe leading to a Narnia of AI solutions. Let's highlight some of the benefits that make them so enticing:

1. **Cost-Effective**: With a subscription model, you're only paying for periodic access to services, eliminating the need for heavy upfront investment in AI infrastructure. It's like leasing a luxury car instead of buying it; you get the experience without the exorbitant price tag.
2. **Scalability**: These platforms allow users to scale their AI usage up or down based on their needs. It's a 'pay-as-you-grow' approach, making it perfect for businesses of all sizes.
3. **Access to Latest Updates**: Just like your music app updates its library with the latest hits, subscription-based AI platforms provide regular updates and improvements, ensuring you're always using the most advanced tools.
4. **Diverse Solutions under One Roof**: From machine learning algorithms to natural language processing tools, these platforms offer a wide range of AI solutions under one umbrella, saving users the trouble of dealing with multiple vendors.

Exploring the AI Marketplaces

Now, let's turn our attention to the bustling bazaars of AI, the AI marketplaces. Picture an online marketplace where you can browse, buy, or rent AI models to suit your specific needs. Think of it as an Amazon for AI, a hub where developers, businesses, and AI enthusiasts can come together for a shared purpose.

The Grandeur of AI Marketplaces

AI Marketplaces democratize access to AI by connecting AI model developers with potential users. Here's what makes them the powerhouse of the AI industry:

1. **Access to a Broad Spectrum of Models**: AI Marketplaces offer a diverse range of models designed for different tasks. Whether you're looking for a model to predict stock prices or one to detect spam emails, chances are you'll find it in an AI Marketplace.
2. **Speed up Deployment**: By offering ready-to-use models, these marketplaces reduce the time and resources needed to build and train your own model. It's akin to buying a readymade cake mix instead of baking a cake from scratch.
3. **Monetize AI Skills**: For AI developers, these marketplaces provide a platform to monetize their models and showcase their skills to a global audience. It's their Etsy store for AI!
4. **Trial and Testing**: Many marketplaces allow you to test models before purchasing, ensuring you get a model that's a perfect fit for your needs. It's like trying on clothes before buying but for AI!

AI has assisted the growth of subscriptions in a variety of businesses. But how precisely is artificial intelligence assisting in the advancement of the subscription economy? Why are AI-powered subscription models the way of the future? Subscription services have been so popular in the previous decade that practically every software company is headed in that way. The subscription economy is fundamentally altering the way consumers purchase goods and services, and new subscription-based business models such as Software-as-a-Service (SaaS), Content-as-a-Service (CaaS), and Access-as-a-Service (AaaS) have made it easier than ever for businesses to transition from one-time purchases to recurring revenue models.

AI-powered Subscriptions Are on The Rise

AI is expected to contribute more than $15 trillion to the global economy by 2030 (more than China and India's current GDP combined), implying that its impact across all industries will be enormous in the future years.

AI will benefit retailers of all types (through AI, they will be able to further enhance the user experience, make intelligent recommendations, streamline customer support through chatbots, and create more personalized interactions), but subscription-based retailers (whether they offer physical products or a SaaS-based business model) will benefit the most.

How Artificial Intelligence is Changing the Subscription Economy

There are several ways in which artificial intelligence is assisting the subscription industry's rapid and continuing expansion. Let's look at some of the ways AI is empowering the subscription economy, from improved suggestions to automated customer lifecycle management.

Customer Lifecycle Management Is Being Automated

Managing the client lifecycle, which explains how a customer-to-business relationship matures and progresses over time, is one of the most taxing aspects of running a subscription-based model. Customer acquisition and retention are critical indicators of success in the subscription market (especially the latter). Thus it's critical to manage every stage of the customer lifecycle to keep customers engaged. AI is important in this because it allows subscription firms to automate the management of client lifecycles.

Making Appropriate Recommendations

The most significant job of AI in subscription services is to provide each consumer with individualized recommendations. AI enables businesses to collect data from customers, analyze that data, and use the insights gained from that data to make intelligent, relevant recommendations that address a customer's most pressing needs: this is significant, given that 80% of consumers are more likely to purchase from a company that provides personalized experiences.

Lowering Customer Churn

Customer churn (also known as customer attrition) is the moment at which a client stops using (and so paying for) your product or service. Keeping churn rates as low as possible is critical for subscription businesses because it ensures they retain more consumers in the long run. This is another area where AI can help for a variety of reasons:

- Predicting when churn will occur.
- Investigating why and how churn happens.
- Taking proactive measures to reduce churn.
- Detecting and avoiding unintentional churn.

Increasing the Number of Leads

AI is increasingly being used by B2C and B2B firms to create leads. AI-powered lead generation solutions, in particular, enable the automation of the entire lead generation process for B2B firms: B2B businesses may use AI to identify potential consumers, produce targeted marketing messages for each lead, and distribute those messages across numerous channels.

CHAPTER 5

STRATEGIES FOR EFFORTLESS MONEY-MAKING ONLINE

Tired of the usual 9-5 work and wishing you could make money without having to endure nerve-racking job interviews or being bossed around? Keep your head on because we have some game-changing news for you! Artificial intelligence (AI) is here to transform the way we earn money in this tech-driven era of limitless possibilities. Buckle up and prepare to be blown away by the thrilling world of AI-powered moneymaking tactics.

SCALING AND AUTOMATING ONLINE INCOME STREAMS

Passion and market demand are critical for success in internet entrepreneurship. However, embracing scalability and automation is critical if you want to optimize your earning potential and enjoy time independence. By intelligently implementing these two features, you can achieve new levels of profitability while freeing yourself from time-consuming activities. This section will look at ideas and tactics for achieving financial success and work-life balance.

Scalability

When it comes to exploiting digital products, the potential for scalability is enormous. By generating and selling e-books, online courses, or software, you can reach a large number of people with little extra work. These digital items are simple to copy and supply electronically, allowing you to service several consumers at the same time. When combined with suitable marketing methods and a high-quality product, the earning potential becomes nearly endless.

The Influence of Digital Products

Scalability is a distinct advantage of digital products. In contrast to physical items, which necessitate production, inventory management, and shipping logistics, digital products may be generated once and easily replicated. This means you may sell your digital products to an unlimited number of clients without having to worry about inventory or production costs. With low overhead, you can concentrate on fine-tuning your marketing methods to maximize your earnings.

E-books

E-books have grown in popularity in recent years. They enable authors and subject matter experts to digitally share their knowledge and thoughts. You can establish yourself as an authority and reach a global audience by creating an e-book on a topic of knowledge. You may attract readers from all around the world with the correct marketing strategy, enhancing your earning potential.

Online Courses

Online courses have transformed how individuals learn. They offer a flexible and accessible platform for people to learn new skills and knowledge. You can use your expertise as a content developer to create and sell online courses. You may reach a large audience and earn money from course enrollments by using services like Udemy or Teachable. With the option to scale your course to accommodate thousands of students at the same time, your profit potential can be enormous.

Software

Software is critical in solving various digital needs and issues. By building software solutions for specific challenges, you can produce a product with significant scaling potential. You can reach a large number of people with a productivity tool, a mobile app, or a SaaS (Software as a Service) application. The idea is to find a market need and offer a one-of-a-kind solution that adds value to your users' lives.

Affiliate Marketing

Affiliate marketing is a great way to increase your income potential. As an affiliate, you advertise others' products or services in exchange for a commission on each transaction made through your referral. You can establish passive income streams by leveraging your existing audience or building a focused following. Choosing trustworthy items that connect with the interests and demands of your target audience is critical for affiliate marketing success. You can increase your earning potential and develop trust with your audience by truly suggesting things you believe in.

Recurring Revenue from Membership Sites

Membership sites are a wonderful source of recurring money. Creating a membership-based website and providing exclusive content or services can help you build a dedicated community of subscribers who pay a monthly subscription fee. This concept enables you to produce steady money while providing ongoing value to your subscribers. Scalability is built into the structure of membership sites, allowing you to consistently build your membership base and make more money over time.

Driving Membership Engagement with Exclusive Content

It is critical to attract and maintain members by delivering valuable material that keeps them interested. In-depth articles, videos, webinars, or access to a community forum could all be included. By regularly providing original and engaging material, you can create a dedicated community that understands the benefits of membership, hence increasing your scalability and revenue potential.

WHAT EXACTLY ARE SALES FUNNELS?

Sales funnels are powerful automated systems that guide potential buyers through a preset path. These funnels guide people from first awareness to making a purchase, with each step meticulously planned. You may create email sequences, lead capture pages, and sales pages that function in tandem by leveraging automation tools and platforms.

The Advantages of Sales Funnels

Sales funnels provide numerous benefits to businesses:

Conversions have increased:

You can maximize conversions at each stage of the customer experience by properly building your sales funnels.

Sales funnels work automatically once set up, decreasing the need for manual intervention and saving up time for other important duties.

Nurturing Customer Relationships:

By automating regular processes, you can spend more time cultivating relationships with potential consumers, providing individualized attention, and providing a great customer experience.

Sales funnels enable you to adjust your messaging and offers based on where clients are in the funnel, enhancing relevancy and engagement.

Using Automation to Improve Your Sales Funnels

To get started with sales funnels, take the following steps:

Identify Your Target Audience:

Learn about the demands, pain issues, and goals of your target customers. This understanding will help you create content and offers for each stage of the funnel.

Create Interesting Content:

At each level of the funnel, create interesting and informative content that resonates with your target audience. To engage and guide prospects, use a combination of articles, videos, social media posts, and emails.

Improve Your Landing Pages:

Make sure your lead-capturing and sales pages are well-designed and conversion-optimized. To optimize efficacy, test features such as headlines, calls-to-action, and forms.

Streamline Your Email Sequences:

Create automated email sequences to give valuable material, nurture leads, and gently guide them into purchasing.

Iterate and analyze:

Analyze the success of your sales funnels on a regular basis and make data-driven modifications. Analytic tools can be used to discover bottlenecks, optimize conversions, and improve overall efficacy.

MAXIMIZING REVENUE WITH EFFECTIVE PRICING MODELS

AI (artificial intelligence) is transforming many elements of business, including pricing methods. The ability of AI to analyze large quantities of data and generate predictions can be game changers when it comes to determining the proper price for items or services. Using AI can result in more dynamic, customer-focused, and successful pricing models. Here are some examples of how artificial intelligence might assist in increasing income through smart pricing models:

Dynamic Pricing

Artificial intelligence systems can analyze massive amounts of data in real-time, including market trends, competition prices, customer behavior, and seasonal demand. Using this data, AI may dynamically alter prices to optimize revenues and ensure competition. E-commerce enterprises and airlines, for example, frequently employ AI-based dynamic pricing to alter their products depending on real-time demand and competition prices.

Personalized Pricing

Individual client data can be analyzed by AI to provide customized pricing. AI can recommend an optimal price that a customer is likely to accept based on their purchasing history, behavior, and preferences. Personalization has the potential to boost sales and consumer pleasure.

Value-Based Pricing

AI can assist firms in implementing value-based pricing by studying customer behavior, preferences, and willingness to pay. It can determine which features or services customers most value and are willing to pay a premium for. This enables businesses to price their goods or services based on perceived customer value rather than just covering costs or matching competitor prices.

Predictive Pricing

Based on previous data and current market conditions, AI can forecast future price trends. This can assist firms in setting prices that maximize future revenues. For example, AI can foresee a rise in demand for a product, allowing the corporation to raise prices in advance.

Price Optimization

AI algorithms can assess the effects of alternative pricing models on sales and earnings. Based on this study, AI can recommend the best pricing to optimize revenue or profit. This type of price optimization can significantly boost a company's bottom line.

Subscription Pricing

AI may assess consumer usage habits and preferences in order to recommend the best subscription plans. A streaming provider, for example, could utilize AI to offer a plan based on a customer's viewing patterns. This can lead to increased client satisfaction and retention.

Discount Management

Discounts can be a strong tool for increasing sales, but they can also eat into profits if not carefully managed. AI can examine the impact of discounts on sales and profitability and recommend the best discount rate to increase sales while maintaining profits.

AI-enhanced pricing models have the potential to greatly boost a company's revenue and profitability. However, when adopting AI in pricing, organizations must also consider the ethical and regulatory ramifications. Transparent disclosure regarding the use of AI in pricing can help establish customer trust and ensure regulatory compliance.

CONTINUOUS INNOVATION AND ADAPTATION IN THE ONLINE LANDSCAPE

The online world is a constantly evolving environment characterized by constant innovation and the necessity for organizations to react quickly to changing trends. Companies must constantly alter their strategy to remain competitive as digital technologies advance and consumer behaviors shift. Here are some ideas for how firms might develop a culture of continuous innovation and adaptation in the internet world:

Adopt Agile Practices

With its iterative and incremental approach, the agile methodology enables firms to react quickly to changes. Teams can constantly analyze their performance, learn from their triumphs and mistakes, and adapt their tactics based on real-time input by working in sprints.

Spend Money on Research and Development

To keep up with technology breakthroughs and market trends, businesses should invest extensively in R&D. Having a specialized team dedicated to researching new technologies, analyzing user behavior, and designing innovative solutions can help firms stay ahead of the competition.

Promote an Experimentation Culture

Inspiring people to take calculated risks and experiment with new ideas can result in game-changing discoveries. Companies should foster a climate in which failure is perceived as a learning and growth opportunity rather than a setback.

Make use of Data and Analytics.

Data-driven decision-making can assist organizations in remaining competitive in the internet environment. Companies can get insights into their innovation strategy by studying user data, market trends, and competition actions. Businesses can also use predictive analytics to foresee future trends and adjust their tactics accordingly.

Concentrate on Customer-Centered Innovation

Businesses should prioritize ideas that benefit their customers. Businesses that understand their customers' demands and pain areas can create solutions that directly address these concerns, boosting their value proposition and building client loyalty.

Continuous Learning and Training

Businesses must invest in constant learning and training programs for their personnel as technology evolves. Teams can better adapt to the changing online scene and promote innovation by remaining up to date on the newest tools, methodologies, and best practices.

Work with External Partners

Collaboration with other companies, startups, academic institutions, or even customers can provide new views and spark innovation. Collaborative efforts can result in the development of game-changing solutions that would not have been achievable otherwise.

Encourage Internal Entrepreneurship

Intrapreneurship, or enabling employees to act as entrepreneurs within the organization, can be a significant engine of innovation. Employees who are given the freedom and resources to develop their ideas can greatly contribute to a company's innovative skills.

In today's fast-paced online world, adaptability is essential. Companies must stay adaptable and willing to change their strategy, operations, or even company models in reaction to market movements or technological advancements.

In the changing internet landscape, continuous innovation and adaptation are critical for survival and success. Businesses may survive in the digital environment by cultivating an innovative culture, harnessing data, focusing on customer-centric solutions, and remaining open to change.

CHAPTER 6

BUILDING A BRAND AND MARKETING STRATEGY

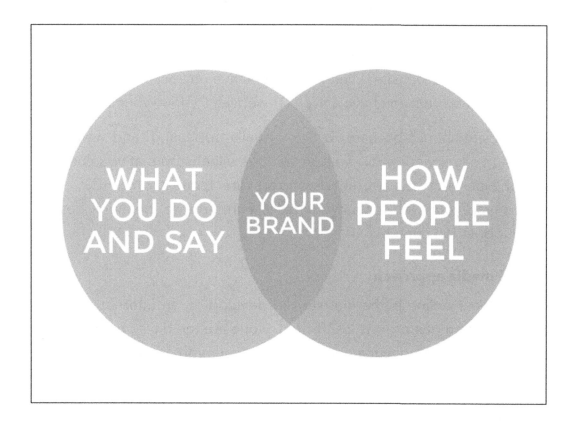

A solid online presence is critical in today's digital age for obtaining success in the online money-making sector. With billions of people using social media and the emergence of influencer culture, businesses and individuals can use these powerful tools to connect with their target audience, build credibility, and drive income. This chapter digs into social media marketing strategies and influencer collaborations, offering ideas and techniques for building a strong online presence.

ESTABLISHING A STRONG ONLINE PRESENCE

The digital age is arrived! There is no doubt that having your business online is not a luxury but a necessity. Building an online presence, on the other hand, entails more than simply developing a platform for customers to visit. To build your business, you must do things correctly.

So, how do you get noticed on the internet? Certainly, details range from one company to the other. Some businesses may wish to focus on direct conversions, while others may want to provide knowledge and instruction. Whatever your objective is, it will be meaningless if no one can find you online. Here are some helpful hints for developing a solid web presence.

5 Ways to Establish a Powerful Online Presence

Create a visually appealing website.

Every company requires a website. Even if you are active on social media, your popularity will not translate into money until you have a five-star website to drive your sales.

An excellent website should be easy to use, visually appealing, and well-suited to driving conversions. Using a knowledgeable web developer will ensure that you construct a platform that will pique the interest of the consumers who are directed to it. CMS, SEO, eCommerce, and other tools can help your website run optimally. Furthermore, beautiful design is essential across all of your branded content.

Plan your social media approach.

Getting your business online is the first step in developing an internet presence. However, simply being present on platforms is insufficient. Gone are the days of publishing on the same day and delegating social media management to your summer intern. If you want to get ahead in today's world, you must plan ahead.

CE Banners (840x104)

The best method to integrate your business goals with your online presence is to develop a strong, concise, and visually appealing social media plan. A social strategy has several aspects, such as posting hours, SEO, content calendars, and so on. Hiring a reputable agency will assist you in navigating the new world of social media and getting you and your company to the top of everyone's feed.

Media creation

Instagram, Facebook, TikTok, and LinkedIn are among the most media-focused social sites. Even Twitter accounts benefit from a solid aesthetic strategy, so don't skip this stage.

Even if your objective is to drive visitors to your website, you must ensure that you have an appealing landing page for customers, and the easiest way to do so is to employ amazing visual assets. Strong video, photo, and graphic design content is the most effective approach to drawing consumers into your marketing funnel. Not a media guru? Employ a professional team! Delegation is never an embarrassing game.

Paid Advertisements

The use of the internet for advertising has created numerous new marketing opportunities. Having an online presence is the first step in spreading the word about your product or service, but using a paid advertising approach can significantly increase your visibility.

Paid ads produce results that organic growth cannot match. Because online ads are less expensive than traditional print, TV, or radio advertisements, they are an inexpensive and worthwhile option for businesses. Furthermore, using paid advertisements allows you to easily market across platforms using simple integration approaches. Check out our blog for more in-depth information on paid advertising methods.

SEO

SEO is an abbreviation for Search Engine Optimization, and it assists your company in ranking high in search engine results. When people are looking for businesses or products these days, they virtually always turn to the internet for assistance.

Everyone wants their company to be the first search result and to attract the most qualified consumers. The most effective way to accomplish this is to use SEO. Creating a solid SEO plan can help your website perform better in searches and ensure that you are reaching your target market. SEO is a continually changing landscape, so remain current on the latest developments.

SOCIAL MEDIA MARKETING AND INFLUENCER STRATEGIES

Social media marketing and influencer strategies have transformed the way individuals and organizations connect with their target audiences and drive online revenue in today's digital landscape. Social media platforms have evolved into effective tools for increasing company visibility, encouraging customer participation, and generating leads. This chapter delves into the ideas and strategies of successful social media marketing, as well as how to leverage influencers to optimize the impact of your online money-making activities.

Marketing on social media

Creating an Effective Social Media plan: A solid social media plan is the bedrock of effective online marketing. It entails building a complete plan adapted to specific platforms and intended outcomes, as well as defining clear goals and objectives, identifying target audiences, and developing a comprehensive plan tailored to specific platforms and desired outcomes. You can maximize your social media presence and increase audience interaction by choosing the correct content formats, publishing schedules, and engagement strategies.

Utilizing Different Social Media Platforms:

Because each social media site has its own set of traits and demographics, it is critical to grasp the dynamics of each platform. Facebook, Instagram, Twitter, LinkedIn, and YouTube all have their own set of best practices and user preferences. Customizing your content and interaction techniques to match the platform's unique characteristics provides optimum efficacy and reach.

Creating Engaging and Shareable material:

Creating engaging and shareable material is essential for attracting your audience's attention on social media. Visual design, compelling captions, and storytelling tactics are critical components in developing material that is appealing to your target audience. Encouraging user-generated content and allowing social sharing can help you naturally extend your audience and cultivate brand champions.

Building and Nurturing a Social Media Community:

Long-term success in social media marketing requires cultivating an engaged community of followers. You may develop a devoted and supportive community by encouraging active involvement, conversations, and feedback through comments, likes, shares, and direct messaging. Exclusive content and incentives can help to increase engagement and brand loyalty.

Strategies for Influencers:

Influencer Marketing: Harnessing the Influencer's Power:

Influencers are important in social media marketing because they use their influence and credibility to promote businesses and products. Identifying relevant influencers in your area and forming genuine relationships that connect with your brand values and target audience can increase brand recognition and drive customer acquisition. Influencer initiatives, such as sponsored content or brand endorsements, can significantly increase your reach.

Measuring and Analyzing Social Media effectiveness:

It is critical to track the effectiveness of your social media marketing activities in order to optimize your methods. Using social media analytics tools and establishing key performance indicators (KPIs) can provide insights into engagement, reach, conversions, and other pertinent metrics. Analyzing this data allows you to make data-driven decisions and fine-tune your social media marketing strategy.

CHAPTER 7

NAVIGATING LEGAL AND REGULATORY CONSIDERATIONS

Navigating legal and regulatory considerations is critical for individuals and enterprises engaging in online money-making activities in the digital age, where information flows freely, and data is a valuable asset. This chapter delves into the legal framework surrounding online activity and highlights the essential factors that must be addressed in order to assure compliance, preserve intellectual property, and uphold ethical standards.

INTELLECTUAL PROPERTY RIGHTS AND AI

The rapid evolution of artificial intelligence (AI) is pushing the boundaries of many disciplines, and intellectual property law is no exception. As AI gains the ability to generate creative content and make inventions, it raises significant challenges for existing intellectual property rights (IPR) frameworks. These challenges necessitate a deep dive into the interplay between AI and IPR, revealing the need for adaptive legal structures that can accommodate the future of AI-driven creations.

AI and Patents

Patents serve to protect the rights of inventors, granting them exclusive rights to their inventions for a certain period. However, when an AI system invents, determining the rightful patent holder becomes a complex issue. The current legal frameworks in many jurisdictions insist that an inventor must be a human, sidelining the growing capabilities of AI.

Take the case of the AI system DABUS, which made headlines when it was credited with inventing a food container and a warning light. The UK Intellectual Property Office and the European Patent Office denied the patents on the basis that DABUS, as an AI, could not be an inventor. Contrarily, South Africa granted the patent, becoming the first country to officially recognize AI as an inventor. This ongoing global debate underscores the imperative for a comprehensive reevaluation of patent laws to accommodate AI-made inventions.

The Complexity of Copyright Laws in the Context of AI

Copyright laws traditionally protect the creative expressions of human authors. But as AI systems generate increasingly sophisticated creative outputs, the application of these laws becomes less clear-cut.

Consider the "Next Rembrandt" project, where an AI was trained to analyze Rembrandt's style and subsequently generated an original artwork that mimicked the master's style. Who should hold the copyright for such an artwork? Is it the AI for creating the work, the programmers who developed the AI, or the team that initiated and oversaw the project? This scenario further illustrates how current IPR laws are ill-equipped to handle the implications of AI-generated content.

Trade Secrets and Transparency in AI

Trade secrets, an essential aspect of intellectual property, have taken center stage with the advent of AI. Companies often guard their AI models and algorithms as trade secrets, creating a veil of opacity around the workings of AI systems.

This lack of transparency can be problematic, especially in sectors like healthcare and finance, where AI-based decisions can significantly affect individuals. The tension between protecting trade secrets and promoting AI transparency poses ethical and legal dilemmas, highlighting the need for revised regulations that strike the right balance.

Redefining IPR for the AI Era

AI's impact on intellectual property rights is undeniably significant, prompting a much-needed reevaluation of existing laws. As AI continues to make strides in creativity and invention, it's crucial that IPR frameworks evolve in tandem. There is an urgent need for legislation that recognizes the role of AI in creation and invention while also protecting the rights of human creators and fostering transparency in AI systems.

Navigating the intersections of AI and IPR is no simple task. It demands thoughtful deliberation, international cooperation, and a willingness to adapt existing norms. As we advance further into the AI era, it becomes increasingly clear that our legal frameworks must be as innovative and adaptive as the technology they aim to regulate.

DATA PRIVACY AND COMPLIANCE IN ONLINE VENTURES

In the era of digital ubiquity, data has emerged as a new form of currency. As businesses leverage data to drive decisions, enhance user experiences, and gain a competitive edge, they must also navigate the delicate landscape of data privacy and compliance. In the world of online ventures, this balance is pivotal, involving a complex interplay of technical, legal, and ethical dimensions. This in-depth exploration unravels the essence of data privacy and compliance in online ventures and underscores their profound significance in today's digital world.

The Increasing Importance of Data Privacy

Data privacy refers to the right of individuals to have their personal data protected from unauthorized access and misuse. As online ventures collect and process vast amounts of user data, they bear the responsibility to safeguard this information and ensure its use aligns with the established privacy norms.

From cookies tracking browsing behaviors to personal information provided during account creation, data privacy affects every facet of a user's online experience. Respecting and preserving this privacy is not only an ethical obligation for businesses but also a legal requirement under various national and international regulations.

Data Compliance

Compliance in the data context refers to adherence to data protection laws, regulations, and standards. These regulatory frameworks govern how businesses collect, store, process, and share personal data. They also mandate specific procedures in the event of a data breach. Non-compliance can result in hefty fines and reputational damage.

For online ventures operating across borders, compliance becomes even more complex, as they need to comply with the data protection laws of all the regions they operate in. These might include the General Data Protection Regulation (GDPR) in the European Union, the California Consumer Privacy Act (CCPA) in the United States, and the Personal Data Protection Act (PDPA) in Singapore, among others.

Striking the Balance

While data is an invaluable resource for online ventures, using it responsibly and in compliance with regulatory standards is critical. Businesses must adopt privacy-by-design approaches, where data privacy considerations are embedded in every stage of their data handling processes, from collection to storage and utilization.

Businesses can use techniques such as anonymization and pseudonymization to de-identify personal data, ensuring it cannot be linked back to the individual it was collected from. This allows them to extract insights from the data without compromising privacy. Encryption is another vital tool to protect data during transmission and storage, preventing unauthorized access.

Data Privacy and Compliance

Data privacy and compliance are no longer optional for online ventures; they are fundamental to their operation and survival. As data protection laws continue to evolve and tighten worldwide, businesses must stay ahead of the curve, proactively updating their privacy policies and data handling practices.

Moreover, privacy and compliance should not be seen as burdens but rather as opportunities to build trust with customers. Transparency in data practices and rigorous adherence to privacy standards can enhance brand reputation and customer loyalty. After all, in an age where data breaches are all too common, a commitment to data privacy can be a powerful differentiator.

CONCLUSION

As we reach the end of this book, it's important to remember that we stand at the threshold of a new era. In the same way that our understanding of nutrition has profoundly changed the way we look at food and health, our understanding of AI and, more specifically, prompt engineering is reshaping the world of business, technology, and beyond.

Throughout this exploration into the depths of AI and prompt engineering, we've traversed the intricacies of crafting effective prompts, unraveling the mysteries of the revolutionary GPT-4 model, and learning how to harness this power to carve out profitable online ventures. I hope that this journey has left you with the tools and understanding needed to navigate the ever-evolving AI landscape with confidence and innovation.

Remember, the AI revolution is not about man versus machine. Rather, it's about how man and machine can collaborate for the betterment of society, businesses, and personal lives. Only our imaginations are restricted by AI and prompt engineering. It's our responsibility to employ these tools ethically, ensuring that while we profit and prosper, we also safeguard the privacy, security, and overall well-being of individuals and communities.

It is an exciting time to be part of the AI revolution. The opportunities for growth, innovation, and profit are abundant and growing. However, as the science of AI evolves, so must our approach to leveraging it. The importance of lifelong learning, adaptation, and innovation cannot be overstated in this context.

Let the knowledge gained from this book not be the end of your learning but rather a starting point. Let it inspire you to continue exploring, experimenting, and embracing new challenges in the realm of AI and prompt engineering. Each chapter was designed to be a stepping stone, paving the way for you to become an integral part of this incredible revolution.

The AI frontier is wide open, and the promise of success is there for those willing to master these new tools and techniques. As we move forward, I look forward to seeing the incredible innovations and achievements you will bring to this exciting field.

Made in the USA
Las Vegas, NV
28 July 2024